SUMMER OF FU

A Chronicle of Hurricane Cha

An Unforgettable Chapter
in the History
of Sanibel and Captiva

Written by Jim George
Photo Journal by Jim Anderson

Published by
Pelican Wing Publications, LLC
1577 Sand Castle Road
Sanibel, Florida 33957
Phone: 239-472-0168 Fax: 239-472-2094
E-Mail: jmaphotography@cs.com

Cover Photo:
Hurricane Charley
Friday, August 13, 2004
Courtesy Of National Oceanographic and
Atmospheric Administration (NOAA)

1

FOREWORD

The term "hurricane" took on new meaning in the summer of 2004. Floridians were held hostage and the nation's attention was riveted as a tropical storm, Bonnie and four major hurricanes – Charley, Frances, Ivan and Jeanne – made landfall in the State of Florida within a space of six weeks, causing more than $42 billion in damage, destroying 25,000 homes, leaving thousands more homeless or without jobs and exacting a human toll of 117. Throughout Florida, few escaped the wrath of nature in that summer of fury. One in every five homes was damaged, and insured losses exceeded $20 billion. With each wave of destruction, Florida communities shook the dust from the rubble, even as the threat of the next storm loomed, and began the task of rebuilding not only their torn and devastated structures, but in many cases their shattered lives.

What had begun as an idyllic summer ended with over a million people fleeing their homes in fear of their lives. This book chronicles – in words and pictures – a barrier island community's response to the effects of one of those storms, Hurricane Charley; the action of officials and the community spirit in the aftermath.

Jim George
Author

Jim Anderson
Photo Journalist

INTRODUCTION

Hurricane Charley was born as a tropical wave off the coast of Africa in early August of 2004. The barrier islands of Sanibel and Captiva were more than a thousand miles away nestled in the blue-green waters of the Gulf of Mexico just three miles off the coast of Fort Myers, Florida. Considering the distance the storm would have to travel, the islands presented a miniscule target. Many unrelated events would have to converge in order to bring the storm to the shores of the islands.

Barrier islands are no more than sand dunes pushed up a few feet above sea level by millennia of ocean currents. They have no protection from storms. By definition they are barriers themselves, designed by nature to act as breakwaters for the mainland against wind and tides. Sanibel and Captiva had been lucky over the years. Given the number of storms that, had hit Florida or spun into the Gulf of Mexico, the two islands had been luckily spared. Only a few had touched them, most at a time when the islands were sparsely populated and undeveloped. The storms of 1921 and 1926 literally shaped the islands. The storms breached Captiva, separating it into two islands, creating Redfish Pass. Those storms destroyed the islands' character as farming communities due to the over-wash of saltwater, precipitating their growth into one of the world's most popular destination resorts.

Hurricane Donna in 1960 was the last large storm to strike the islands and cause major damage, but that was three years before the construction of the Sanibel Causeway. Significant development had not yet begun. In 1992 Hurricane Andrew, one of the most deadly storms to ever strike Florida, threatened Sanibel and Captiva, but it, too, passed harmlessly by many miles out in the Gulf. In the years since, a parade of storms has threatened. Minor damage was sustained on several occasions. With the passing of each uneventful hurricane season, however, the memory of the destructive force of a hurricane dimmed. The devastation of Hurricane Donna became a footnote in the history of the islands.

Each year emergency management officials and weather forecasters pleaded with residents to heed instructions and make the necessary storm-evacuation preparations. The complacency of many people was summed up in the comments of one Sanibel resident, who, when faced with Hurricane Charley's mandatory evacuation order by public officials, elected to stay on the island with his 10 year old daughter, "in our own home... to enjoy the hurricane," a storm that would eventually reach Category 4 status with predicted 130 mile per hour winds and a tidal surge of 18 feet. One hundred people on Sanibel and 20 people on Captiva made that same decision and but for a quirk of nature, they survived because the storm made an unexpected last-minute turn, and the 18-foot storm surge did not materialize.

As 6,000 island residents and visitors fled to the safety of the mainland, the islands grew quiet. Even the birds appeared to be seeking shelter. The silence was broken only by the whisper of the first breezes heralding the hurricane. The gray bands of clouds that preceded the eye of the hurricane by hundreds of miles began to appear the morning of the storm and reached like twisting tentacles, grasping the blue blanket of sky. Gradually the day grew darker. As the storm built in intensity after having devastated Jamaica and the western tip of Cuba, the marvel of satellites and television stunned anxious island residents who had sought protection at motels or shelters on the mainland. Others were miles away in Northern residences as they watched the storm turn toward the Southwest Florida coast and away from the predicted landfall in the Tampa Bay area. Along with Sanibel city officials, who two days before had established a temporary command post at the Bell Tower Holiday Inn on the mainland, the whole community could only wait and watch as hour by hour it became apparent that their worst fears would become a reality.

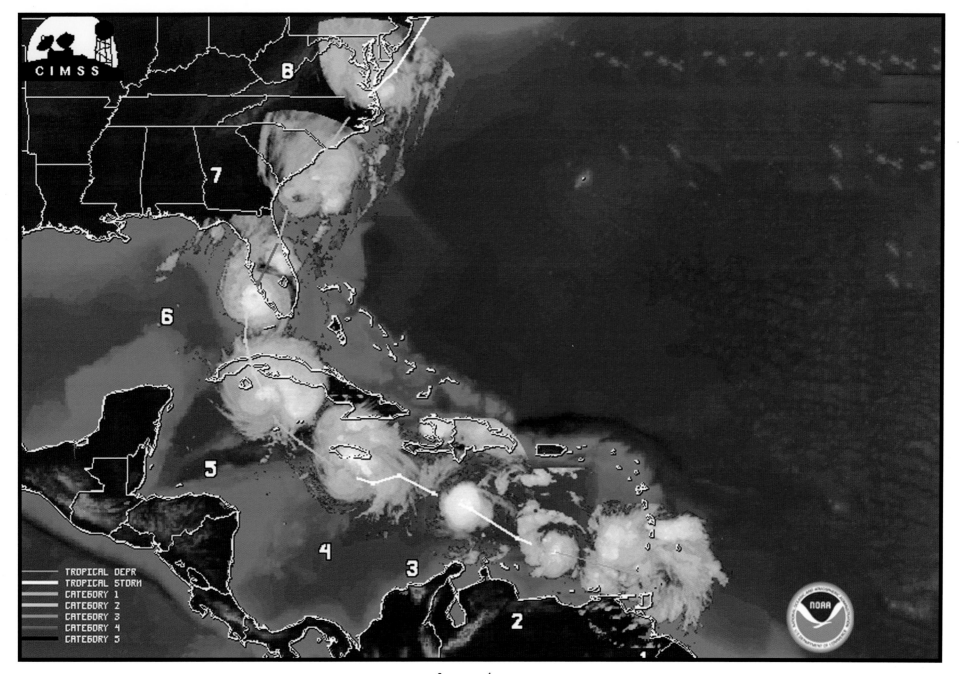

CIMSS

TROPICAL DEPR	
TROPICAL STORM	
CATEGORY 1	
CATEGORY 2	
CATEGORY 3	
CATEGORY 4	
CATEGORY 5	

Photo Montage Of Hurricane Charley's Track

Photo Courtesy Of National Oceanographic and Atmospheric Administration (NOAA)

A QUIET BEGINNING

The summer of 2004 was a typical Florida summer – hot, humid and sticky. Hordes of mosquitoes brought in by late afternoon showers only added to the discomfort. The heat and humidity drove the tourist to other destinations. Part time residents had gone back to their other communities. Restaurants were being enjoyed without long lines; traffic, though still heavy, was not congested. The pace of life had settled into an unhurried, casual rhythm.

Warm southeasterly breezes swept in from the Gulf of Mexico. The shimmering heat that hung over the beaches baked the sand and ratcheted the Gulf water temperature up into the 80s. The barrier island chain which extends from Sanibel on the southeastern tip to Cayo Costa on the northern end, lies three miles off the mainland. In summer they are sunlit havens collecting gentle breezes that are never felt deep inland. That same geography, however, makes the low lying island chain vulnerable to storms.

The hurricane season had officially started on June 1. By August, tropical weather activity had remained uneventful. Islanders were going about their business or pleasure with the usual background noise – the news of war in Iraq was not good, presidential elections were just around the corner, the stock market was in limbo, the City of Sanibel was mired in controversy with Lee County over replacement of the drawbridge – and no one was paying attention to the weather except to complain about the heat.

While all eyes were turned toward the south Atlantic in search of the first signs of activity, Tropical Depression One formed right in Sanibel's own backyard 175 miles off the coast of Charleston, South Carolina, on July 31. There was no real threat to Florida, but the trough of low pressure associated with the weather system created heavy rains over Southwest Florida, which was already saturated from heavy rains the prior week. Although there were no areas reporting flooding, Lee County Commissioners declared a local seven-day emergency to prepare for flooding in some sections of the county. The northeast sections of the county recorded four inches of rain. Tropical Depression One was named Alex and became the first hurricane of the 2004 season on Tuesday, August 4. Its center was just off the coast of Wilmington, North Carolina.

Before The Storm – Aerial View Of The Sanibel Lighthouse

7

Weather Advisory

*ON THAT SAME DAY, 2,000 MILES AWAY, A TROPICAL WAVE EMERGED OFF THE AFRICAN COAST...
HURRICANE CHARLEY WAS STIRRING IN THE WOMB OF MOTHER NATURE.*

Meanwhile, Hurricane Alex veered northeast into the Atlantic. It reached maximum winds of 120 miles per hour just Southwest of Cape Race, Newfoundland, on August 5 before it weakened into a tropical storm. It continued its eastward path and ultimately struck the United Kingdom.

On August 2, two days after Hurricane Alex formed, Tropical Depression Two was born deep in the south Atlantic, but it never reached full-fledged hurricane status. Winds of less than 75 miles per hour relegated the weather system to only Tropical Storm status. From the moment it was born east of the Lesser Antilles, the track of the storm gave no indication of a Florida landfall. As it entered the Gulf of Mexico by the weekend of August 6, its course indicated an almost straight line toward the coast of Texas, well off shore and south of Sanibel and Captiva.

Monday – August 9

A steamy morning... The air was heavy with moisture even as the sun came up. Pelicans dipped over the Gulf in their wild uncoordinated dive for bait fish as the coldly efficient osprey circled overhead. With its telephoto vision, the osprey watched for that almost imperceptible movement below the surface of the water which would trigger a screaming dive and almost certain death for an unlucky fish. As the sun rose higher, shellers were scattered along the beach in familiar stooped position hoping for a junonia or lions paw, the ultimate reward for hundreds of hours of searching. Traffic on the Sanibel's main thoroughfare, Periwinkle Way, was just beginning to flow with the usual influx of workers and visitors.

Confusion is usually the hallmark of the first back-to-school day, but the Sanibel School children were unusually orderly on that Monday. School officials would voice their amazement at how smooth the day had gone and hoped it boded a successful school year.

Dave Roberts, weather consultant for the City of Sanibel, didn't feel good about the weather system he was watching. It was unusual for a tropical disturbance to be so far south at that time of year – an oddity he thought. The warm surface

Sunset Beach At Redfish Pass, Captiva

9

conditions and the overall environmental conditions, he reasoned, would probably push the disturbance toward western Cuba and then into the Gulf of Mexico. His morning e-mail to the city would reflect that concern.

Rising at 4 a.m. was part of Sanibel Deputy City Clerk Pam Smith's usual routine. With an hour drive to Sanibel City Hall from her home on the mainland, she passed the riding time monitoring a weather station. On that morning Smith heard a report of a weather system deep in the Atlantic. Old habits were hard to break. Having spent 10 years in emergency management in North Carolina, she was keenly alert to weather during the hurricane season. After arriving at her office, she checked two weather Web sites and saw the disturbance mentioned on the radio, but attached no significance to it at the time.

Sanibel Police Chief Bill Tomlinson was looking forward to the day as he arrived at City Hall. With his blonde hair and boyish features, the burly veteran of 20 years in law enforcement looked more like a college linebacker than a seasoned cop. There were staff issues to attend to that morning, but his usual practice was to quickly scan his messages and e-mail. His computer monitor blinked with each new message as he rapidly clicked through them. An e-mail from Dave Roberts, the city's weather consultant, slowed his pace. Roberts' e-mail was reporting a tropical disturbance southeast of Grenada. Roberts, affectionately known by city staff as "Doppler Dave," was expressing only mild concern about the location of the weather system. It was unusual that a tropical depression would be that far west and south at that point in the season. No big deal, Tomlinson thought. Yet, as he left his office for a meeting, a disquieting feeling stirred inside him, borne out of his many years in emergency management. His instincts and training always elevated his stress level during the hurricane season, and storms even a thousand miles away were always worrisome. The city's detailed hurricane plan had been updated in June. It mobilized every agency and department. Tomlinson felt a measure of comfort in that knowledge, but gnawing at a tiny corner of his mind was the reality that the five-year-old plan had never been tested in a major storm.

The plan would be the key element in guiding all emergency activity over the next three weeks. Lee County was divided into 10 zones, each with its own hurricane plan coordinated by a central facility – the Lee County Emergency Operations Center. Sanibel and Captiva comprised Zone 10. The chief of police for Sanibel and the fire chiefs of Sanibel and Captiva would share command of the zone. The plan had seven phases; initial tracking, hurricane watch, hurricane warning, imminent landfall, hurricane landfall, recovery and return to normalcy. Each phase would trigger a new level of activity beginning with the fifth day prior to an estimated strike. The fifth day prior in this case was August 9.

Beautiful Beaches Of Sanibel

Although he was doing routine tasks, Tomlinson's mind already was on phase one. This included early preparation such as shuttering windows, finding barricades for streets and securing contracts for debris removal. Public notification and alerts would not begin unless later reports by Roberts indicated a need for greater concern. These thoughts were paramount in Tomlinson's mind as he headed toward a special meeting called by City Manager Judie Zimomra. Zimomra also had received the Roberts e-mail and was initiating the first phase of the hurricane plan. From that point on, City Hall became a beehive of activity, in a very deliberate and organized mode. Each individual and department had a specific checklist of activities, and the countdown had begun. Zimomra had a high degree of confidence in the staff's ability to carry out the plan.

Sanibel Police Major Mike Murray, director of emergency operations for the city, also had been monitoring Roberts' weather report. Like Tomlinson, Murray was not feeling a high level of anxiety over the report but was nervous about it, nonetheless. A discussion with Roberts had left him unsettled. In his four years in emergency management and 20 years in law enforcement, Murray's instincts were honed to a fine-edge, instincts he had learned not to ignore.

Ten miles further north on Captiva Island, which is separated from Sanibel by Blind Pass – a sliver of water a mere hundred yards across – Captain Jay Halverson, second in command of the Captiva Fire Department, was mentally organizing his day. Fire Chief John Bates was out of town for the week. The tiny station house, nestled in among the trees and eclectic wooden structures of that island paradise was, until Bates' return, his responsibility. On that day there hadn't been a single rescue or fire call. Equipment still had to be checked and cleaned anyway. Halverson was aware of the position of the storm, and he, like Tomlinson, was beginning to go through the mental process of the hurricane plan.

By now Tropical Depression Two had moved from the Caribbean into the Gulf of Mexico as a named tropical storm, Bonnie, and was racing on an unswerving line toward a predicted landfall somewhere along the coast of Texas. It was far offshore of Sanibel and Captiva and posed no threat to the islands.

Sanibel Fire Chief Rich Dickerson brought his staff together early that morning to review the hurricane plan. The first order of business was to make certain personnel were ready. In his 22 years of fire service, Dickerson had a lot of close calls; but with the storm so far away, he wasn't too concerned.

The Morning After Charley

Heron Checking The Damage

Sanibel Causeway

Lighthouse Fishing Pier

13

Meanwhile, local NBC TV meteorologist, Robert Van Winkle was routinely tracking the weather system. Jim Reif, chief meteorologist for Waterman Broadcasting and ABC TV in Fort Myers, was on a much needed vacation in Myrtle Beach, South Carolina, on his way to Philadelphia. Both stations are owned by Waterman Broadcasting and operate out of the same studios. Reif had been uneasy about the season. He knew that the area was in the final year of a 10-year cycle of above average storm activity. In June he had commented to Van Winkle about the quietness of the season. Van Winkle recalled that Reif had speculated back in June that, by August 15, all hell was going to break loose and everything would start up. Alas, the seeds of the hell Reif had envisioned were already being sown deep in the south Atlantic.

After seeing the early advisories and following the progress of the storm on his laptop computer as he traveled, Reif realized that he may not finish his vacation but continued north, anyway, in hopes that conditions might change. Both Reif and Van Winkle had reached the same conclusion; there would be a storm threat to the area, although it was still too early to speculate on the size or power of it. "We knew from the computer models that the storm would be within a 200 mile track of this area," Reif said, "which means there was a chance it might hit somewhere in our neighborhood." Van Winkle recalled that there was a fleeting moment when the storm may have "sneaked" beneath a trough of weather that would have pushed it to Mexico or Texas.

Only three weeks before, Rob Jess, refuge manager for the J.N. "Ding" Darling National Wildlife Refuge, the federally owned 7,000-acre pristine mangrove estuary on Sanibel, had signed off on the new, updated version of the refuge hurricane plan. The refuge, managed by the U.S. Fish and Wildlife Service, had substantial resources at its disposal – people, heavy equipment, sawyers and boats – all invaluable in an emergency. When Jess put his signature to the plan, he didn't realize how soon the plan would be tested. Although officials were feeling the first pangs of concern, to others on the islands it was just another normal summer day. As morning eased into early afternoon, the heat lay like a blanket on the islands.

Sand Castle Road - The Dunes

Trees Uprooted, Just Missing Houses

Australian Pines Damaged Many Structures

Most Pool Enclosures Did Not Survive

National Hurricane Center Weather Advisory, August 9, 1:45 PM

INTERESTS IN THE EASTERN AND CENTRAL CARIBBEAN SEA SHOULD CLOSELY
MONITOR THE PROGRESS OF THIS SYSTEM.

AT 145 PM AST... 1745Z... THE CENTER OF TROPICAL DEPRESSION
THREE WAS LOCATED NEAR LATITUDE 11.7 NORTH... LONGITUDE 61.1 WEST OR
ABOUT 50 MILES... 80 KM... SOUTHEAST OF GRENADA.

THE DEPRESSION IS MOVING TOWARD THE WEST NEAR 22 MPH...
35 KM/HR... AND THIS GENERAL MOTION IS EXPECTED TO CONTINUE FOR
THE NEXT 24 HOURS.

MAXIMUM SUSTAINED WINDS ARE NEAR 35 MPH... 55 KM/HR... WITH HIGHER
GUSTS. SOME STRENGTHENING IS FORECAST DURING THE NEXT 24 HOURS.
THE DEPRESSION COULD BECOME A TROPICAL STORM TONIGHT OR ON TUESDAY.

Hurricane Charley was born as Tropical Depression Three near the Windward Islands in the South Atlantic, a thousand miles from Sanibel. The fateful week had begun. Many lives were destined to change. No one could have predicted the fury that nature would visit upon the State of Florida, a fury that would touch virtually every household, every individual and test the inner strength of thousands. Soon many would be homeless, and some would not survive.

Tuesday – August 10
As the sun came up over Sanibel and Captiva, Tropical Storm Bonnie was reaching a point 390 miles south of the mouth of the Mississippi River with sustained winds of 50 miles per hour.

"I can't explain it," Pam Smith said when recalling the initial advisory on Tropical Depression Three, "but there was something about this storm that worried me even though it was a thousand miles away." She again had watched the weather report before going to work. It unsettled her. When she arrived at work, she told the city manager that this was the storm that was going to hit Sanibel. "It was a feeling I just couldn't shake," she said. Smith began her part of the hur-

The Majority Of Damage Was To Roofs And Pool Enclosures

ricane plan by packing essential city records. She also was alerted by the Lee County Emergency Operations Center that it might be mobilizing shortly. Under the hurricane plan, Smith would be the city's liaison at the center.

When Fire Chief Dickerson came in that morning, his mind was clicking through the various elements of the hurricane plan. He wanted to set up a meeting with the City of Sanibel's Mike Murray and "Ding" Darling's Rob Jess. They had to consider where an off island command post would be located. He wanted to move some personnel, along with an engine and an emergency vehicle, to the Island Water Association facility. Other equipment had to be moved to the mainland. Dickerson's thinking still hadn't reached the level of full evacuation of the island.

Chief Tomlinson arrived at police headquarters with the same nagging worry about the storm that he had the day before. He had watched the TV weather broadcasts on the prior evening; they had reinforced his concern. Roberts' new e-mail indicated the same storm track as the day before. As Tomlinson read the e-mail, a basic precept of emergency management kept blinking in his mind's eye: always assume the worst and plan accordingly.

National Hurricane Center Weather Advisory, August 10, 11 a.m.

```
TROPICAL DEPRESSION THREE UPGRADED TO TROPICAL STORM BULLETIN
TROPICAL STORM CHARLEY ADVISORY NUMBER 5
NWS TPC/NATIONAL HURRICANE CENTER MIAMI FL
11 AM AST TUE AUG 10 2004

...CHARLEY CONTINUES MOVING RAPIDLY WEST-NORTHWESTWARD OVER THE
CARIBBEAN...

AT 11 AM AST...THE GOVERNMENT OF JAMAICA HAS ISSUED A TROPICAL STORM
WATCH FOR JAMAICA.

INTERESTS IN AND AROUND THE CENTRAL AND NORTHWEST CARIBBEAN SEA
SHOULD CLOSELY MONITOR THE PROGRESS OF THIS SYSTEM.
```

Concrete Poles Snapped

Power Lines Down Everywhere Posed A Safety Hazard

```
AT 11 AM AST... 1500Z... THE CENTER OF TROPICAL STORM
CHARLEY WAS LOCATED NEAR LATITUDE 13.7 NORTH...
LONGITUDE 68.3 WEST OR ABOUT 350 MILES... 560 KM...
SOUTH-SOUTHEAST OF SANTO DOMINGO IN THE DOMINICAN REPUBLIC.
CHARLEY IS MOVING TOWARD THE WEST-NORTHWEST NEAR 24 MPH ... 39 KM/HR... AND
THIS GENERAL MOTION IS EXPECTED TO CONTINUE FOR THE NEXT 24 HOURS.

MAXIMUM SUSTAINED WINDS ARE NEAR 45 MPH... 75 KM/HR... WITH HIGHER
GUSTS. SOME STRENGTHENING IS FORECAST DURING THE NEXT 24 HOURS.
```

Lee County's Office of Emergency Management director, John Wilson, was in Sarasota at a conference of emergency managers when he heard of the storm's potential threat. The National Hurricane Center placed a conference call to those in Sarasota also to discuss the storm. Wilson immediately made plans to return to Lee County. Twenty-five years in emergency management had stirred his instincts. On his way back to Lee County, he, too, kept thinking of how unusual it was for a storm to make landfall on the west coast of Florida in August. Typically, that would happen in September or October. That fact offered a ray of hope. What troubled him was that the National Hurricane Center, in this case, had made a radical shift from its normal forecast and was, indeed, predicting a possible west coast landfall.

Wilson would learn later that a confluence of weather events was building which would affect historical weather patterns. The Bermuda high pressure system that affects the weather over Florida was a lot further east at this point. The combination of the Bermuda high coupled with a low pressure system over the state created a funnel effect which would pull the storm across the state. In addition, an unusual cold front had come through in August; that created driving currents which ultimately affected the course of the hurricane.

Island activities continued at a normal pace that day: City Council delayed a vote on whether or not to drop its lawsuit against Lee County to prevent replacement of the causeway drawbridge... the County Commission approved raising the causeway tolls to $6; the City of Sanibel reached agreement with the state to allow licensed alligator hunters to "harvest" alligators four feet in length or greater; and former Sanibel mayor and now Congressman Porter Goss had been named the new director of the CIA by President George W. Bush.

However, the first signs of storm preparation on the island became visible along Periwinkle Way, as some businesses began

Unlucky Place To Park Car In The Dunes

Recliner Came Out Of Loggerhead Cay Window
On Other Side Of Building

Portable Toilet On Captiva

Roofs Peeled Off Of Moonshadows Condos
On Middle Gulf Drive

installing shutters and covering windows. The island beaches remained active; beachgoers showed no apparent concern about the approaching storm. Supermarkets on the islands and the mainland experienced slightly higher activity as people began stocking supplies.

Sanibel and Captiva officials and employees were ramping up hurricane preparations.

Weatherman Jim Reif continued to monitor the storm while he was traveling. He realized he would have to return to Fort Myers. The approaching weather system, he told himself, portended big trouble for Southwest Florida.

Wednesday- August 11

The 8 p.m. advisory on Tuesday depicted the storm moving rapidly west, northwest across the central Caribbean and gaining strength. The message from Sanibel's weather consultant, Roberts, at 8 a.m. had not been encouraging. "I knew it would hit the island," Roberts said later. "There was a serious risk, and all I could think of was, thank God Sanibel was reacting accordingly. I knew the magnitude of the prediction I was making, but Sanibel was probably one of the best prepared cities in the country."

Refuge Manager Jess and his staff decided at 8:30 a.m. on Wednesday to treat the storm as a Category 4 hurricane, even though at this point it was still a Category 1. "It was a gut instinct," Jess said, attributing it to his Cherokee heritage. "It wasn't any one thing. I just knew it was going to hit here. Being half Native American, I've always been receptive to my instincts. If we were wrong, it only would have meant we lost some time; but if we were right, we'd be ready." All along, Jess had been in touch with city officials coordinating refuge activity.

Many people would mention the feeling, instinct, intuition or foreboding about the storm hitting Sanibel – even though it was so far away – but none could articulate why "that" particular storm or "that" particular year. All would say they had not experienced such a feeling in past storms. This collective consciousness was pervasive.

The Lee County Emergency Operations Center triggered partial mobilization of the Geographical Response Division which activates the 10 geographical emergency zones in the county. Each zone would have a twice- daily conference call with the center. They would follow a time- delineation schedule from that point on, a scripted plan with detailed steps. The center was beginning to work through the various stages of the plan; in effect, it was putting all resources on standby. At full mobilization, the center would house 75 people.

Chief Dickerson implemented phase two of the Sanibel Fire Department's plan and began the process of rotating personnel to be sure they were rested in case the storm hit. He continued to receive calls and faxes on the weather status from the City of Sanibel. At 10 a.m. he participated in a State Emergency Operations Center conference call to discuss the statewide situation.

Captiva Fire Captain Halverson was alert to the advisories and following the storm track. Halverson was in constant telephone communication with Chief Bates. The storm track was already disrupting air travel into Florida, and Bates was having difficulty arranging a return. Captiva, like Sanibel, was rotating personnel in order to assure that everyone was rested in the event the storm hit.

By Wednesday Police Major Murray's main concern was securing the island and getting as many people off the island as possible in case an evacuation was ordered. The bottom line for his job as emergency management director was to assure there would be no injuries or fatalities.

Sanibel City Manager Zimomra's regular 9 a.m. staff meeting was devoted entirely to the storm preparations during which she expressed her expectations of the staff and city employees. Pam Smith once again voiced her prediction that the storm would hit Sanibel. She said the storm reminded her of Hurricane Floyd, which had hit North Carolina twice in 1999. The plan for establishing the temporary City Hall and command center on the mainland was discussed. Rooms for the temporary City Hall and for city employees already had been booked at the Holiday Inn in Fort Myers.

National Hurricane Center Weather Advisory, August 11, 11 a.m.

BULLETIN, 11 AM EDT WED AUG 11 2004

```
TROPICAL STORM CHARLEY ADVISORY NUMBER 9
NWS TPC/NATIONAL HURRICANE CENTER MIAMI FL...
CHARLEY NEARING HURRICANE STRENGTH...

A TROPICAL STORM WARNING AND A HURRICANE WATCH REMAIN IN EFFECT FOR JAMAICA.

A HURRICANE WARNING REMAINS IN EFFECT FOR THE CAYMAN ISLANDS.

AT 11 AM EDT...1500Z... THE GOVERNMENT OF CUBA HAS ISSUED A
HURRICANE WATCH FOR THE FOLLOWING PROVINCES OF WESTERN CUBA...
ISLE OF YOUTH.

A HURRICANE WATCH REMAINS IN EFFECT FOR THE FLORIDA KEYS FROM DRY TORTUGAS TO CRAIG KEY.
A HURRICANE WATCH MEANS THAT HURRICANE CONDITIONS ARE POSSIBLE WITHIN THE WATCH AREA...
GENERALLY WITHIN 36 HOURS. ADDITIONAL WATCHES WILL LIKELY BE REQUIRED FOR PORTIONS OF
THE FLORIDA PENINSULA LATER TODAY.

AT 11 AM EDT...1500Z... THE CENTER OF TROPICAL STORM CHARLEY WAS
RELOCATED NEAR LATITUDE 16.5 NORTH... LONGITUDE 76.1 WEST OR ABOUT
110 MILES... 175 KM... SOUTH-SOUTHEAST OF KINGSTON JAMAICA.

CHARLEY IS MOVING TOWARD THE WEST-NORTHWEST NEAR 18 MPH
...30 KM/HR... AND A GRADUAL TURN TO THE NORTHWEST IS EXPECTED DURING
THE NEXT DAY OR SO. ON THIS TRACK THE CENTER WILL BE MOVING NEAR
THE SOUTH COAST OF JAMAICA LATER TODAY.

MAXIMUM SUSTAINED WINDS ARE NEAR 70 MPH...110 KM/HR... WITH HIGHER
GUSTS. CHARLEY IS EXPECTED TO BECOME A HURRICANE LATER TODAY.
```

At a meeting with the Fort Myers Beach city manager later, Zimomra was restless and anxious to get back to Sanibel. She knew that preparations were in full swing. There was no turning back on the execution of the hurricane plan unless the storm took a major turn from its predicted path. "We were in full evacuation mode," Zimomra said.

National Hurricane Center Weather Advisory, August 11, 2 p.m.

2 PM EDT WED AUG 11 2004

... CHARLEY BECOMES A HURRICANE... RAIN BANDS SPREADING OVER
JAMAICA...

A TROPICAL STORM WARNING AND A HURRICANE WATCH REMAIN IN EFFECT
FOR JAMAICA.

Meterologist Jim Reif reached Atlantic City, New Jersey on that Wednesday, and booked a flight back to Fort Myers. He arrived at 4 p.m. and was on the air for the five o'clock broadcast. Both Reif and Van Winkle knew at this point that the hurricane would affect the entire west coast of Florida, even though computer models still indicated a more northerly track. Hurricanes are not pinpoints, but affect large areas. High winds and storm surge were inevitable. It was just a question of the exact landfall point. "One of the weaknesses of hurricane forecasting is the inability to predict the explosive power or intensification of a hurricane," Reif said. The track can be followed on a path which weather maps show as a "cone of uncertainty," meaning the storm could strike anywhere within that cone. Reif and Van Winkle drew some comfort from history. They knew that, by and large, when storms come off the western tip of Cuba in August, they rarely turn east. At that point they were assuming that it was merely a question of how far off shore the storm would pass the Southwest Florida coast.

Storm preparations were now frenetic all over the islands as businesses boarded up windows. Although there hadn't been a mass exodus off the islands, traffic to the mainland just seemed to dwindle during the day; day trippers apparently nervous about the preparation, decided that the mainland was a better place to be. Some hurricane-savvy islanders also began their own self-imposed evacuation. The pace of residents shopping for essentials – batteries, water, duct tape, canned goods and flashlights – also picked up.

By now a weather trough along the Texas coast had pushed Tropical Storm Bonnie into an unexpected sharp right (easterly) turn toward the coast of the Florida Panhandle. Satellite photos clearly showed Bonnie approaching the Panhandle as Hurricane Charley was approaching Jamaica.

At 4 p.m. the Lee County Emergency Operations Center placed a conference call to all local EOCs. It included a discussion by the county's weather consultant, who was predicting a Tampa area landfall. Director John Wilson continued to watch the storm. Its consistent track indicated that landfall could be between Tampa and Naples, and he couldn't take the chance that the storm would pass offshore of the Southwest Florida coast. He ordered a mandatory evacuation for the next morning for the barrier islands and coastal areas at risk. He knew that an evacuation order meant disrupting people's lives, but a later order would not give people time if the storm turned toward Lee County.

Zimomra called another staff meeting late that afternoon to review the latest information. Fifteen to 20 people representing all elements of the city's hurricane plan were present. Included were police, fire, public works, Island Water Association, Fish and Wildlife Service, Lee County Sheriff 's Department, city staff members, Community Housing, even representatives of the library. The consensus was to request City Council to declare a state of emergency and initiate evacuation orders. Following the meeting, the city updated its Website with all the latest storm information. The Website would ultimately serve as a key communications tool for residents.

Zimomra called a special city council meeting at 7 p.m., during which she and Chief Tomlinson reported on the progress of the storm and recommended that Council declare, on that day, a state of emergency and voluntary evacuation of anyone with special needs. Mandatory evacuation was to begin at 8 a.m. Thursday morning. The city would proceed with setting up a temporary City Hall and command center at the Holiday Inn in Fort Myers. The city's emergency ordinance was activated. It prohibited the sale of alcohol, established a curfew and forbade price gouging. All police were put on standby. Officially, the city was in full evacuation mode.

Thursday – August 12
Immediately after arriving at the Sanibel fire station at 7 a.m., Dickerson called a staff meeting, and phase three of the plan was initiated. Full mobilization had begun; even though the storm was still a Category 2 and it did not yet require mandatory evacuation of emergency personnel. They would implement their plan to move some of the fire equipment and personnel to the safety of the Island Water building that evening, while moving other equipment to the Edison College campus on the mainland.

Pam Smith, meanwhile, had been called to an early meeting at the Lee County EOC, where they were fully mobilizing. She would be the voice of Sanibel and Captiva at the EOC and the conduit through which all city information would flow to the center. In addition to county emergency personnel, each city had a liaison there. Also included were essential personnel from Lee County, representatives from other government agencies, fire, police, Red Cross, the Health Department, hospitals, media representatives, Department of Transportation and the Southwest Florida Water Management District. All emergency activity in the county would be coordinated from the EOC, which in turn would be in direct contact with state emergency operations, county EOCs from around the state and the National Hurricane Center. After a review of the hurricane track, EOC Director Wilson advised the group that effective at 7 a.m. Friday morning the EOC would go to full 24 hour operation. All personnel would remain at that location until further notice. Pam Smith didn't know it then, but it would be three weeks before she would return to her own home.

Sanibel city employees were still rotating their work and personal responsibilities during the day. Director Mike Murray viewed this as a key aspect of the hurricane plan – one that probably kept employees focused throughout the storm and the recovery. "Everyone was allowed to go home and secure their homes and families and assure their safety before returning to work," he said.

Further north, satellite photos were showing Tropical Storm Bonnie staggering ashore in the Apalachicola area with sustained winds of 50 miles per hour and dissipating over land. Far to the south Hurricane Charley was approaching western Cuba.

National Hurricane Center Weather Advisory, August 12, 11 a.m.

```
BULLETIN
HURRICANE CHARLEY ADVISORY NUMBER 13... CORRECTED
NWS TPC/NATIONAL HURRICANE CENTER MIAMI FL
11 AM EDT THU AUG 12 2004

CORRECTED FOR ADVISORY NUMBER FROM 12 TO 13

...CHARLEY GETTING A LITTLE STRONGER... HURRICANE WATCH EXTENDED
NORTHWARD ALONG THE FLORIDA WEST COAST...
```

A HURRICANE WARNING REMAINS IN EFFECT FOR THE FLORIDA KEYS FROM THE
DRY TORTUGAS TO THE SEVEN MILE BRIDGE... AND FOR THE Southwest FLORIDA
COAST FROM EAST CAPE SABLE TO BONITA BEACH. THE WARNING WILL LIKELY BE EXTENDED
NORTHWARD LATER TODAY OR TONIGHT. A HURRICANE WARNING MEANS THAT
HURRICANE CONDITIONS ARE EXPECTED WITHIN THE WARNING AREA WITHIN THE NEXT 24 HOURS.
PREPARATIONS TO PROTECT LIFE AND PROPERTY SHOULD BE RUSHED TO COMPLETION.

AT 11 AM EDT...1500Z... THE HURRICANE WATCH HAS BEEN EXTENDED NORTHWARD ALONG
THE FLORIDA WEST COAST TO THE SUWANNEE RIVER. THE HURRICANE WATCH IS NOW IN EFFECT
FROM NORTH OF BONITA BEACH TO THE SUWANNEE RIVER. A HURRICANE WATCH MEANS
THAT HURRICANE CONDITIONS ARE POSSIBLE WITHIN THE WATCH AREA... GENERALLY WITHIN 36 HOURS.

A TROPICAL STORM WARNING REMAINS IN EFFECT FOR THE FLORIDA KEYS FROM THE SEVEN MILE
BRIDGE TO OCEAN REEF... AND ALONG THE SOUTH FLORIDA MAINLAND FROM OCEAN REEF TO EAST CAPE
SABLE... INCLUDING ALL OF FLORIDA BAY. A TROPICAL STORM WATCH MAY BE REQUIRED FOR PORTIONS
OF THE FLORIDA EAST COAST LATER TODAY.

A HURRICANE WARNING REMAINS IN EFFECT FOR THE CAYMAN ISLANDS.

AT 11 AM EDT...1500Z... THE GOVERNMENT OF CUBA HAS ISSUED A HURRICANE
WARNING FOR THE FOLLOWING PROVINCES OF WESTERN CUBA... PINAR DEL RIO
...LA HABANA... CIUDAD DE LA HABANA...MATANZAS... AND THE ISLE OF YOUTH.

AT 11 AM EDT...1500Z... THE GOVERNMENT OF JAMAICA HAS DISCONTINUED
ALL WARNINGS FOR JAMAICA.

AT 11 AM EDT...1500Z... INFORMATION FROM RECONNAISSANCE AIRCRAFT
AND RADAR FROM CUBA INDICATE THE CENTER OF HURRICANE CHARLEY WAS
LOCATED NEAR LATITUDE 19.7 NORTH... LONGITUDE 81.2 WEST OR ABOUT
25 MILES... 40 KM... NORTH OF GRAND CAYMAN.

CHARLEY IS MOVING TOWARD THE NORTHWEST NEAR 17 MPH... 28 KM/HR.
A TURN TO THE NORTH-NORTHWEST IS EXPECTED LATER TODAY.

The 11 a.m. advisory offers a little hope in that the storm was forecasted to turn to the north-northwest – a possibility that it might turn away from the Southwest Florida coast and perhaps pass by well offshore.

During the course of the day the City of Sanibel phoned each residence and business advising them of the mandatory evacuation. Lee County Electric Cooperative began moving equipment off the island during the day, and Island Water personnel evacuated to the Holiday Inn at 10 p.m.

By now Reif and Van Winkle knew that Southwest Florida would feel hurricane force winds and storm surge. They were broadcasting on a 24-hour schedule. At 1 p.m. Hurricane Charley became a Category 2 storm just after passing Grand Cayman.

National Hurricane Center Weather Advisory, August 12, 8 p.m.

AT 8 PM EDT...0000Z... THE CENTER OF HURRICANE CHARLEY WAS LOCATED NEAR LATITUDE 21.7 NORTH...
LONGITUDE 82.3 WEST OR JUST EAST OF THE ISLE OF YOUTH CUBA. THIS IS ALSO ABOUT 90 MILES...
145 KM... SOUTH OF HAVANA CUBA.

CHARLEY IS NOW MOVING TOWARD THE NORTH-NORTHWEST NEAR 17 MPH... 27 KM/HR.
A GRADUAL TURN TOWARD THE NORTH IS EXPECTED DURING THE NEXT 24 HOURS.
ON THE FORECAST TRACK... CHARLEY IS EXPECTED TO PASS NEAR HAVANA LATER TONIGHT OR EARLY
FRIDAY MORNING... AND THEN MOVE INTO THE SOUTHEASTERN Gulf OF MEXICO. WEATHER CONDITIONS
SHOULD CONTINUE TO DETERIORATE OVER WESTERN CUBA DURING THE NEXT FEW HOURS.

MAXIMUM SUSTAINED WINDS ARE NEAR 105 MPH... 165 KM/HR... WITH HIGHER
GUSTS. THIS MAKES CHARLEY A CATEGORY TWO HURRICANE ON THE SAFFIR-SIMPSON HURRICANE SCALE.
ADDITIONAL STRENGTHENING IS FORECAST DURING THE NEXT 24 HOURS AND CHARLEY COULD BECOME A MAJOR
HURRICANE LATER TONIGHT OR FRIDAY.
STORM SURGE FLOODING OF 10 TO 14 FEET CAN BE EXPECTED ALONG THE

```
SOUTH COAST OF CUBA NEAR AND EAST OF WHERE THE CENTER MAKES
LANDFALL. IN ADDITION... STORM SURGE FLOODING OF 2 TO 4 FEET... ALONG
WITH LARGE AND DANGEROUS BATTERING WAVES... CAN BE EXPECTED IN THE
FLORIDA KEYS. STORM SURGE FLOODING OF 10 TO 13 FEET IS ALSO POSSIBLE NEAR
AND SOUTH OF THE WHERE THE CENTER CROSSES THE FLORIDA WEST COAST.
```

For the first time the weather advisory carried a storm surge forecast. A forecast of a 10- to 13- foot surge would mean inundation of the barrier islands.

Throughout the course of the day, evacuation of Sanibel and Captiva proceeded smoothly. The island was closed to oncoming traffic. Island businesses and residents completed their preparations and, as the day drew to a close, only a few remaining cars straggled across the causeway toward the mainland. The quaint shopping centers along Periwinkle Way, now with boarded up windows, looked more like a street from a third world country than the trendy island community that attracted people from all over the world.

All city personnel that were assigned to the Holiday Inn were there by late afternoon with the exception of those still on the island. Major Mike Murray, Lieutenants Jaime Phillips and Scott Ashby, along with several other police officers, continued to patrol the island until the early hours of Friday morning. Murray recalled that one of the first heavy rain squalls from the outer bands of the storm blew through the island as they were leaving.

Zimomra had met with City Council members individually earlier in the week to refresh them on the hurricane plan. Mayor Marty Harrity left the island late in the afternoon, but not before stopping to see several people he knew who were not evacuating. He made one final effort to convince them to leave, but was unsuccessful. Harrity had been criticized a day earlier for Council's action in ordering an evacuation but he, like the other Council members, knew it was the prudent thing to do. Some of those who remained would communicate with Harrity just prior to the storm making land-fall and ask for help in getting them off the island – help that was no longer available.

Boat Aground At The Green Flash, Captiva

More Davits Failed

Friday – August 13

At 2 a.m., Hurricane Charley passed over Cuba. It left a path of destruction in both Jamaica and Cuba. As the eye moved into the Florida Straits, aerial reconnaissance reported the storm was weakening. By the time Charley reached the Dry Tortugas, it came under the influence of an unseasonably strong pressure trough that had dug from the east-central United States into the eastern Gulf of Mexico. In response to the steering flow on the southeast side of this trough, the hurricane turned north-northeastward and accelerated toward the Southwest coast of Florida. It also began to intensify rapidly.

Arriving at the EOC at 7 a.m., Pam Smith still was absolutely convinced the hurricane would strike Sanibel. Her intuition about it had never wavered during the week.

Rob Jess and all refuge personnel had evacuated the island the night before, but Jess returned Friday morning to handle the last few details and then left the island for the final time at about 10:30 a.m.

By Wednesday night most hotels in the Fort Myers area were booked. Those who planned early were in local hotels. By Friday morning others who had evacuated late were scattered across the state. There was little to do but wait.

"Get off the island and get off now," was Pam Smith's recollection of her phone call to Fire Chief Dickerson in the early morning hours. Hurricane Charley was reaching Category 4 strength, and a storm surge of 15 to 18 feet was predicted. Dickerson phoned EOC's John Wilson. The two had a brief discussion of the impending catastrophe and decided to evacuate all remaining fire personnel to the mainland. There was still a moment of denial as the two men discussed the fact that a Category 4 storm had never made landfall in Southwest Florida in August.

Dickerson attended a 6 a.m. meeting at the Holiday Inn for a final briefing with Sanibel officials. Zimomra, Tomlinson, Murray and all emergency officials present were on high alert, assuming a worst case scenario of a direct hit. Murray commented later that it was the first time in his 20 years as a Sanibel police officer that the staff had to be evacuated. Murray and other officers came back to the island at 7:30 a.m. for a final sweep. They had the names of some individuals who

Jet Ski On Expansive Beach The Morning After

Boat Went Adrift

Davits Gave Way

33

had not evacuated, and one final attempt was made to convince them to leave, to no avail. At 9:30 a.m. Dickerson pulled all remaining fire personnel off the island. Murray left the island at 11 a.m., four hours before the storm would hit. He measured winds of 55 miles per hour on the causeway at that time.

At 8 a.m. Meteorologists Reif and Van Winkle were glued to the Doppler radar. What they saw reinforced their feeling that Southwest Florida was in great danger, even though the "cone of uncertainty" still indicated a more northerly path with landfall in Tampa. They had tracked the storm all night, and for the first time, noted a slightly northeastern track. They watched the storm wobble for more than an hour. Although it's normal for a storm to wobble, their concern at that point was the persistence of the movement toward the northeast.

Shortly after 9 a.m., they made a decision. Without alarming the public, they decided to bring the information to their viewing audience. They were not changing their forecast, which at that time was that the hurricane would pass offshore, but they were concerned about this slight shift eastward which would have grave implications if it persisted.

By 11 a.m. Reif and Van Winkle had a dilemma. The 11 a.m. National Hurricane Center advisory, satellites and reports were showing the storm on a northern track when, in fact, the Doppler radar was telling them it was taking a more north-easterly track. By departing from the hurricane center forecast, they risked confusing their viewers. That could result in people delaying evacuation if necessary. As professional meteorologists, both Reif and Van Winkle knew they could no longer stand behind the National Hurricane Center forecast when they were seeing something different on the Doppler radar. They went on the air and broadcasted their own forecast that the storm would likely hit in the Lee County area.

National Hurricane Center Weather Advisory, August 13, 2 p.m.

BULLETIN HURRICANE CHARLEY SPECIAL ADVISORY NUMBER 18 2 PM EDT FRIDAY AUG 13 2004

CORRECTION... THE TROPICAL STORM WARNING FOR SOUTHEAST FLORIDA FROM
OCEAN REEF TO JUPITER INLET SHOULD BE A TROPICAL STORM WATCH.

... CHARLEY STRENGTHENS TO CATEGORY FOUR HURRICANE AND HEADS FOR SOUTHWEST FLORIDA COAST...

Captiva Drive – The Morning After – A Wall Of Trees Faced Clean-up Crews

35

```
AT 2 PM EDT...1800Z... THE CENTER OF HURRICANE CHARLEY WAS LOCATED NEAR LATITUDE 26.0 NORTH...
LONGITUDE 82.4 WEST OR ABOUT 60 MILES SOUTHWEST OF FORT MYERS FLORIDA.
CHARLEY IS MOVING TOWARD THE NORTH-NORTHEAST NEAR 20 MPH. ON THIS TRACK... THE CENTER OF
CHARLEY SHOULD MAKE LANDFALL IN THE VICINITY OF CHARLOTTE HARBOR FLORIDA LATER THIS AFTERNOON.

MAXIMUM SUSTAINED WINDS HAVE INCREASED TO NEAR 145 MPH WITH HIGHER GUSTS.

STORM SURGE FLOODING OF 10 TO 15 FEET IS EXPECTED NEAR AND
SOUTH OF THE WHERE THE CENTER CROSSES THE FLORIDA WEST COAST.
```

The 2 p.m. National Hurricane Center advisory was at last consistent with what Reif and Van Winkle had been seeing. The eye of the storm was only six miles wide, unprecedented for a hurricane. The tightly packed hurricane was rapidly building in intensity as 145 mile per hour winds swirled around its eye. More importantly, the erratic nature of its movement made it hard to predict where it would make landfall. That surely would complicate the task of emergency managers in their evacuation of the coastline. The Lee County EOC had simultaneously gotten the 2 p.m. advisory.

At 2 p.m., city and emergency officials at the Holiday Inn were convinced that the hurricane would make landfall on Sanibel. City officials and emergency personnel were constantly coming in and out of the room. The seriousness of the situation notwithstanding, City Council members had to be mindful of Florida's Sunshine laws which restrict them from gathering in anything other than a publicly announced meeting.

With the wind howling relentlessly outside their hotel rooms, city officials watched in helpless fascination as the eye of the hurricane approached the shores of Sanibel. The storm was poised off the coast of Sanibel like a crouching cat ready to leap. The unthinkable was about to happen. Dickerson's thoughts flashed to those who had elected to remain on the island. A 15- to 18- foot tidal surge surely would result in fatalities. Most deaths in hurricanes are normally from tidal surge rather than wind, he thought. He began making phone calls in a vain attempt to find body bags. None could be found. Even calls to the county medical examiner were fruitless.

As the storm bore down on Sanibel, Mayor Harrity leaned over to Chief Tomlinson and asked him what he thought

Scenes From Captiva Drive

about what they were seeing. An ashen faced Tomlinson responded, "It's over." The assumption was the island would be leveled. Harrity later recalled that all he could do was close his eyes and say a prayer. "We were helpless," he said.

Judie Zimomra received a phone call from Pam Smith warning her of the impending wall of water; she discussed her fear that the water would level many buildings. Zimomra's major concern, like Dickerson's, was geared toward the more than 100 people who had not evacuated. She expressed her frustration to Smith that there was no way that anyone could help them now.

At this point EOC Director Wilson handed Smith a piece of paper with three words written on it – "Sanibel, 145 mph" – the latest wind measurement as the storm approached the island. With the storm taking dead aim at Sanibel, the tidal surge and the wind velocity spelled certain devastation and fatalities. Smith recalled later that the tension in the room felt like a heavy blanket as the reality of the situation became clear. The storm was no longer an abstract icon on a television screen or computer monitor. In all its fury, it was poised to strike.

At about 2:30 p.m. most of urban Lee County lost electric power, robbing people of their ability to watch the storm's progress. Battery-operated radios would keep them abreast, but it was not the same as watching it unfold on a television screen. Cell phones became the primary communication tool out of necessity. Many land based lines were lost when power ceased. In the wake of the storm, cell phones would be the only way to communicate with anxious relatives and friends, but even they would become unreliable: thousands of calls jammed microwave towers and caused some carriers to interrupt service.

Major Murray was on edge about the storm surge. He, too, worried about fatalities from water more than from wind. The predicted surge would be catastrophic. That edginess would last until the end of the next day, when reports were turned in from all search teams.

As city officials huddled around the TV screens, they noted a slight twitch to the north in the storm's forward motion. Five miles away at Waterman Broadcasting Studios, Reif and Van Winkle were in disbelief, but they were familiar enough

A Boat Found Land At 'Tween Waters Inn

39

with the nature of hurricanes to know that energy within the eye wall may shift periodically from one side to the other, causing it to wobble briefly. Incredulity replaced anxiety. Hurricane winds of up to 110 miles per hour already were lashing the east end of Sanibel – a prelude to the strike – but there was no question now that the storm was tilting to a northerly turn. The next 15 minutes passed like a slow motion movie as the storm slowly veered away from Sanibel. The eye was now skirting just offshore, heading toward Captiva. The strong winds from the hurricane's right wall were buffeting the beach front homes and condominiums as the eye moved parallel to the shoreline of Sanibel. It ripped roofs and siding, blew out windows and tossed trees like pick-up sticks. The damage pattern later indicated that small tornadoes had been dancing along the coastline. The wind sheared the treetops across the island and literally defoliated the dense mangrove forests of the "Ding" Darling Refuge.

Islanders who had not evacuated were not yet aware that they had just been given a reprieve.

Having been born on Sanibel, island resident and businessman, Sam Bailey, had experienced many of Mother Nature's tantrums. Hurricane Charley bore higher winds than Bailey remembered from living through the 1935 and 1944 hurricanes that swept the islands. "Back then we didn't have any warning like we do today," he said. Throughout Charley, Bailey remained at his general store with four employees. He said two policemen came to the store before the storm at the city manager's behest to ask him to evacuate. "It would take more than two policemen to get us off the island," Bailey said. "What saved us was the storm moving so quickly," he hastened to add. Bailey had known about the high storm-surge prediction but didn't think it would happen. After the storm, he made his way to his near-beach home and found a 40- foot- long, four-foot deep trench that the small tidal surge had gouged around the house.

"It was scary when we lost power and the TV," Salli Kirkland said later, "but I would probably do it again." She and husband, Billy, felt secure in their three- level home, which had been built to all the latest Sanibel codes. Even with the predicted storm surge, they felt protected. Two weeks later, however, Billy would say at a Sanibel City Council meeting that staying on the island during the storm was probably one of the worse decisions he ever made. Salli said that, although they had been better off than most by having a gas stove for cooking and a gas generator for air conditioning, the aftermath had been worse than the storm. "Billy went out immediately to help neighbors and the emergency people, and I

A Boat On Captiva Wasn't Even Safe On Its Trailer

started cooking. The workers would need food and so would our neighbors." Several neighbors had ridden out the storm with them; Salli had felt a sense of responsibility toward everyone. Billy would become an active participant in assisting in cleanup.

Natalie Brown had remained on the island, but was oblivious to the drama that was unfolding around her. With an assortment of pets that included cats, dogs and birds, Brown opted to stay behind since most shelters would not allow her pets in. After losing power, Brown was unaware of what went on and that a 15- to 18- foot storm surge had been predicted. "It wouldn't have made any difference," she said, "I wouldn't have left my pets." She said she was not frightened and only noticed after the storm that her pool enclosure had collapsed. Two weeks before the storm, Brown had purchased two generators. "I had a feeling I might need them this season."

Evacuation was never a consideration for Mary and Bob Mitchell. Although they had tracked the storm through the week, its path had not alarmed them. "We had been through this many times before and had evacuated only once, Mary said, "and even that time had been a false alarm." As the intensity of the storm built around them, they felt comfortable that they had taken the necessary precautions the day before in securing their house. The Mitchells had lived through violent weather in California and Oklahoma. When they learned that the storm had built to Category 4 with a predicted surge, they realized their position was more tenuous and that additional precautions would be necessary. "We're high enough off the ground to withstand an 18-foot surge," Bob said. "We're far enough away from the beach; the surge wouldn't be that high here." Surprisingly, as the storm raged, they never lost their telephone connection. Although they were without electricity, they kept receiving calls from concerned relatives and friends from as far away as England. They watched and listened as winds gusting to more than 110 miles per hour whipped their trees into a whirling green dervish of branches and leaves, and each thumping sound outside signaled the fall of another tree. High winds and heavy rain kept them in the house until the following morning, when they would see the surrounding destruction. Fallen trees blocked both front and rear entrances to the house, and Mitchell would have to cut his way through.

Mary Beth Greenplate's most vivid memory was that of the pool enclosure breaking away from the house. Greenplate rode out the storm along with her husband, parents, grandparents and five children ranging in age from two to 12, plus

Just Over Bridge On Captiva Island

House Close To 'Tween Waters, Captiva

Just Before The Turn Near The Green Flash, Captiva

Murmond Lane, Captiva

assorted pets. She felt safe in the new piling house her parents had built three years earlier. Greenplate said they had a fleeting moment of regret about not evacuating, but by then the causeway had already been closed. At the height of the storm, when the winds reached maximum velocity, the children were moved to the elevator shaft as a safety precaution. "We'd do the same thing – not evacuate – if another Category 4 came along," Greenplate said, "but if it was a Category 5, I'd have to think about that."

Captiva Fire Lieutenant Paul Garvey was on the mainland, in touch with volunteer fireman, Mark Wells, who had stayed aboard a 30- foot boat at Captiva's Bayside Marina. Wells, the marina harbor master, described to Garvey the rain of rooftops that, during the height of the storm, had been blown off condominiums at nearby South Seas Resort and were falling around the boat. After learning of the predicted 18- foot storm surge, Wells regretted having not taken his boat up into the protected reaches of the Caloosahatchee River. Garvey cautioned Wells to remain aboard the boat. Wells was no stranger to hurricanes. He had ridden out 10 storms prior to Hurricane Charley. He and wife, Debbie, watched from the boat's rear deck as the storm blew in from the east and pushed the tide in front of it – at a rate of more than two feet in the space of minutes – until the boat was high above the dock where they had been moored. Expecting the full force of the tidal surge yet to come, Wells braced for the worst. As the eye passed about two miles offshore, the wind shifted and water started to flood out of the marina, until the boat was floating just inches off the bottom. Following the storm, Wells made his way to the Captiva fire house to start a generator and assess damage. A trip which normally would have taken five took him over 35 minutes. "There were no landmarks left," Wells said. Would he stay again in a Category 4 storm? "Not hardly," he replied.

Wilson and many of the emergency officials would later describe the survival of those who did not evacuate as just plain lucky. "They did not survive a Category 4 storm," Wilson said." They survived a windstorm. The only people that felt the force of a Category 4 were the people right in the eye. The fatalities we saw in Pine Island and Punta Gorda speak to the real power of the storm. Had the storm not turned away from Sanibel at the last minute, the experience of those who did not evacuate the island would have been far different."

By 3:30 p.m. it became apparent that the storm would cross Captiva or North Captiva. The two islands are separated by Redfish Pass. Once across the barrier islands, the apparent storm path was toward Charlotte Harbor. Reif and Van

Captiva's Chapel By The Sea Weathered The Storm

Chapel-By-The-Sea
INTER-DENOMINATIONAL
Sunday Worship 11·A.M.
The Rev. Dr. ROBERT R. HANSEL
Welcome

Four Months Later

45

Winkle were warning viewers in its path to seek shelter. There was no time left to evacuate.

Captiva and North Captiva had once been connected. A 1921 hurricane permanently breached the island, creating Redfish Pass.

At approximately 4 p.m., packing winds of 150 miles per hour, Hurricane Charley made landfall crossing North Captiva and Cayo Costa. Like a giant knife, the eye wall carved a quarter-mile breach in North Captiva Island and formed a pass where Gulf and bay waters joined. Fortunately, there were no homes in that section of the island. Nevertheless, almost every home on North Captiva Island was damaged, and five were destroyed. It would be more than two months before electric power would be restored. Simultaneously, the strong winds of the eye's easterly wall were raking Captiva. The resort community of South Seas, located on the northern most tip of Captiva, and less than a half mile from where the storm crossed North Captiva, felt the punishing effect of the wind. The eye then crossed Pine Island Sound, devastating the northern tip of Pine Island before heading for Charlotte Harbor.

At about 5:30 p.m. the eye wall struck Punta Gorda and Port Charlotte. The area took the full force of the hurricane. It was officially designated as Ground Zero. The devastation was unprecedented. Businesses and homes were indiscriminately leveled. Whole neighborhoods were destroyed in a matter of minutes. Mobile homes were tossed like matchboxes. Roofs and walls were sheared away as though sliced by a razor. The storm then continued across the central part of the state near Kissimmee and Orlando and decreased to a Category 2 hurricane. By the time the eye crossed the east coast of Florida near Daytona Beach at about 11:30 p.m., it left 25 of Florida's 67 counties as designated federal disaster areas.

At 8 p.m. Lee County Sheriff's Deputies Alan Falde and Joe Pappalardo, who are stationed on Captiva, cautiously picked their way across the Sanibel Causeway from the mainland in a four-wheel drive cruiser to determine if there was a land route to Captiva. Crossing the causeway was risky. No one knew at that point whether the causeway bridges were damaged. After safely making the causeway crossing to Sanibel, the two officers could travel only a quarter mile on Periwinkle Way before encountering a wall of fallen trees and vegetation that completely sealed off the main road. Attempts to drive along the Gulf side road, the only other land route, also failed. They would have to fall back on their alternate plan of accessing Captiva by boat. The pair returned to the central command at the Holiday Inn and reported their findings to

After The Eye Of The Hurricane Passed Within Two Miles Of South Seas Resort

Zimomra, Tomlinson and Dickerson. Recovery operations would begin just a few hours later. From that point on sleep would become a rare commodity for all those involved in emergency operations. Adrenalin driven and dedicated to the recovery operation, many would not sleep for the next 48 hours. Henceforth, all would function with only a few stolen hours of sleep and rarely, if ever, give in to their fatigue.

"As bad as it had been in Punta Gorda, we were still very lucky," said Reif, as he reflected later on Hurricane Charley. "The eye of the storm was only five to eight miles wide and it went from a Category 1 to Category 4 very quickly. Had the eye been the size of Hurricane Frances or moved with the slow, lumbering speed of Hurricane Jeanne, the result would have been catastrophic, not only to the barrier islands but coastal communities as far south as Marco Island." Reif said the most significant thing about Hurricane Charley was that the tidal surge was only four feet and never reached the predicted 18 feet. "If it had, it would have washed over the barrier islands and rushed far inland into communities like Fort Myers, Naples and Cape Coral, affecting the entire urban area of both Lee and Collier counties."

There were three factors, Reif explained, that prevented the surge; the size of the eye was only six miles across, the storm was moving rapidly and the storm peaked at the last minute. "Had it traveled hundreds of miles as a Category 4 hurricane, it surely would have built a wall of water in front of it. The longer the wind is blowing, the more time the surge has to build up. Fortuitously, the storm happened quickly."

The same day – August 13 – that Sanibel was being hammered by Hurricane Charley, Tropical Storm Danielle developed south of the Cape Verde Islands in the eastern Atlantic. Over the next week it would develop into a Category 2 hurricane. Tropical Storm Earl developed the very next day – August 14 – in the central tropical Atlantic, but it never reached hurricane strength. Neither storm would threaten the United States, but it was clear that storm activity was escalating.

Evidence Of Wind Velocity On Captiva

THE AFTERMATH

Saturday – August 14

In the 4 a.m. darkness, Deputies Falde and Pappalardo, along with Captiva Fire Department's Captain Jay Halverson and Lieutenant Alan Delameter, pushed their boat off from the Punta Rassa boat ramp at the Sanibel Causeway and headed for Captiva. They knew from the quick foray across the causeway the night before that the land route to Captiva was impassable. The darkness would make the journey by boat treacherous; they did not know what debris might be in the water as they moved up the Intercoastal Waterway.

It took almost two hours for the Captiva team to reach the South Seas Bayside Marina at the northern most tip of Captiva, a journey that ordinarily would have taken 20 minutes. Halverson described the scene as eerie. Daylight was just breaking and in the half light of dawn the team could see that the tree line had been devastated. Buildings that were once shielded from view were now clearly visible. They could barely make out the damage to the buildings at South Seas in the semi-darkness, but as the sun rose, it was evident. Roofs were gone, windows blown out, the once manicured golf course was covered with sand from the tidal surge and vegetation and trees lay shattered and broken in every direction the eye could see. Their job would be to work their way down the island while other teams would work from the southern end at Blind Pass where Sanibel and Captiva were connected by a bridge. The Blind Pass end of Captiva would prove to be the most daunting. The initial teams found a solid wall of broken trees on Captiva Drive, the island's main artery. The huge felled pine trees that lined both sides of the road posed an insurmountable obstacle to passage. Worse, the road was so narrow there was no place to put debris once it was cut. Until the road was open, the only way to move from one end of Captiva to the other would be along the beach in four-wheel-drive vehicles.

As the Captiva boat moved away from the Punta Rassa dock, another boat with a Sanibel team also was pushing off. Since all roads on the island were blocked, the plan was to go by water to the Tarpon Bay Marina just a few minutes away on the bay side of Sanibel and try to reach City Hall, about a mile from the marina. The group included Police Sergeant Mike Cooper, Tony Balog, Mike Henry and Randy Wright from the Public Works Department and Bert Smith, information

Land's End Village At South Seas Resort, Captiva

director for the city. After landing at Tarpon Bay, the group scaled the fence surrounding the property and made its way to City Hall. Cooper remembered thinking, as he stepped off the boat, that not knowing what to expect was like stepping on the moon for the first time. Cooper's and Smith's assignment was to reinstate city systems – computer, telephone and radio communications. They started a generator to activate the city's computer system and police radios, which then enabled communication with the temporary City Hall at the Holiday Inn in Fort Myers. Balog, Henry and Wright were to retrieve heavy equipment from the Public Works Department and begin clearing an access to City Hall and the main road. Then as a gesture that the city had survived and was ready to rebuild, Cooper and Smith raised the flag that had been taken down before the storm.

Simultaneously, Tim Barrett, training officer for the Sanibel Fire Department was organizing nine three-man search teams in the parking area of Tanger Factory Stores, two miles from the causeway toll booth. Under the hurricane plan, the island had been divided into nine zones. Each team comprised of fire, police and sheriff – would be the first to enter the island. Each zone would be individually searched to ascertain that people were safe. Concurrently, a Unified Command Center would be established on the island a short distance off Causeway Road.

The unified command was a concept that had been used by fire departments for years; a concept that was utilized effectively during the World Trade Center tragedy of September 11, 2001. The command, comprised of a representative from each agency, would guide and coordinate the emergency operation so that every time an incident was reported, the proper agency would be quickly dispatched or the necessary resource acquired. Tim Barrett was the incident commander. In addition to Barrett, other members of the command included Police Lieutenant Jaime Phillips, Assistant Fire Chief Danny Duncan, Police Lieutenant Scott Ashby and Utility Specialist Matt Fannon. The Unified Command handled all incidents and logistical issues that arose.

"The Unified Command was the action part of our hurricane plan," Police Chief Bill Tomlinson said, adding, "In this case, we also brought in a liaison to work with the Public Works Department, with Lee County Electric Co-op and the Forestry Service." The group communicated with the Island Water Association and the Captiva Fire Department by radio. The command expanded well beyond the original five individuals, which is the basic concept of unified command. It

South Seas Resort Golf Course – The Pin Still Standing Ready For Play!

incorporates planning, logistics, operations and finance and includes all levels of expertise.

The search teams were awestruck by the tree devastation. Many streets were not passable. There was no access to the interior of the island. Periwinkle Way, the island's main thoroughfare, over which towering Australian pines had formed an almost perfect canopy, was decimated. The canopy of trees was gone. Power lines were strewn among the fallen trees, making for hazardous conditions. The pine trees had been the subject of controversy for years. Many residents had been concerned that the trees would block evacuation in a storm. Hurricane Charley proved them right – once the storm began, fallen trees blocked anyone trying to exit the island. Others who had thought the trees formed an intrinsic part of the island's character would brook no discussion of felling them. So the argument dragged on through the years, finally to be decided by Mother Nature: in one fell swoop she toppled most of them. One official remarked that, had it not been for the Australian pines, residents would have re-entered the island within two days. Unless the streets could be cleared, recovery would be hampered, and the return of residents further delayed.

"The second day was when all the resources started pouring in," Barrett recollected, " and emergency crews would begin the huge task of clearing the roads and restoring the island in a slow block-by-block process." The Unified Command, as well as the work crews were on the island at 5 a.m. each day and worked until as late as 8 p.m. Most worked the first 48 hours without any sleep at all.

At 6 a.m. "Ding" Darling's Rob Jess could not reach any of his staff since all communication was out. He and his 19 year-old son trailered a boat across the causeway to the Sanibel boat ramp and proceeded to Tarpon Bay Marina, which is part of the refuge property. His plan was to do an assessment for Lee County Electric and the Sanibel Police Department. After landing and hiking to Sanibel-Captiva Road, father and son were picked up by a couple that had remained on the island and was driving around looking at the damage. Attempts to go down Periwinkle Way and West Gulf Drive were thwarted by felled trees. Downed live power lines also blocked large areas of San-Cap Road. Jess finally was able to reach the refuge area for a damage assessment. A wind meter located there indicated winds of 148 miles per hour had struck maintenance buildings and blown huge doors off. Those doors were never found. The pattern of tree destruction indicated that two tornadoes had passed through as well, a fact later confirmed by aerial reconnaissance. Jess described going through areas where it was too dangerous to pass because Australian pines were still falling. He would later report

Sunset Beach Looking Across Redfish Pass To North Captiva

his assessment to the command center. The Fish and Wildlife Service already was mobilizing personnel, a force that would eventually number 106 people comprised of sawyers from the Forestry Service, equipment operators, maintenance workers and law enforcement from 10 different states. The Fish and Wildlife Service had three objectives; provide law enforcement to secure the water perimeter, clear debris from the roadways and clear all power lines in order for Lee County Electric crews to restore the electrical grid. Sawyers from the Fish and Wildlife Service assisted in cutting through the vegetation that blocked every roadway. Local businessman, Henry Nachtsheim had stored a huge earth mover on the island and immediately began pushing trees off the roads. Officials referred to Nachtsheim as a "Godsend" in their efforts to clear the roads. By now the city was receiving offers of assistance from municipalities and agencies statewide. The cities of Gainesville and Baldwin had officers on Sanibel within 48 hours.

Sam Bailey opened Bailey's General Store at 7 a.m. and was surprised to see a few people there only minutes later, people who, in turn, were equally surprised that the business was open. No electric power meant that none of the computerized cash registers was operating so, according to Bailey, "We were back to the old days of a paper and pencil and a shoebox." Prior to the storm, Bailey had stocked up on ice. He made it available to anyone who needed it. He also offered work crews whatever provisions they required.

Once the exhilaration of riding out the storm wore off, the people who had stayed, awoke to a sunny morning and the realization that life would be no picnic. Although many had telephone communications, there was no water, no sewer and no power, therefore no air conditioning or lights or working refrigerators or ice. The island was in shambles, with trees down and power lines hanging like Christmas tinsel on downed trees. Roads were impassable; in many cases people could barely exit their own homes. They also learned that if they left the island, they would not be permitted to return. A strict curfew was in effect, and all access to the island was barred.

Those who rode out the storm on the mainland found themselves with a different set of problems. Most of urban Lee and Collier counties – over 300,000 people in Lee County alone – had been without power since about 2:30 p.m. the day before. Without air conditioning, hotels and motels were stifling in the August heat and humidity. Traffic signals were not operating. The traffic that spilled onto the streets – as the heat forced people out to look for water, food and ice – was

North Captiva – The Gap In The Island Brought On By A Previous Storm Widened Ten Fold By Charley

queued up at every major intersection. Within 24 hours, ice would become a precious commodity on the mainland although ironically it was never in short supply on Sanibel. Many had evacuated the islands expecting to return within a day and thus had provisions and clothing for only a short period. Without power, restaurants and fast food establishments were closed. Most supermarkets were open for business, but were not selling food that had been in freezers or coolers, for fear of contamination. Those who did not plan ahead by topping off gas tanks were faced with shuttered service stations; they could not operate pumps without power.

Information coming into the Sanibel Command Center at the Holiday Inn from the County Emergency Operations Center was indicating fatalities in Bokeelia on Pine Island just north and east of Sanibel. Judie Zimomra couldn't help but reflect on the previous day's track change in the storm, away from Sanibel. Had that not occurred, she thought, Sanibel might have the same situation. In fact, she told herself, fatalities could still be a possibility until the last reports of the search teams came in. She felt guilty for feeling good that the eye of the storm had missed Sanibel, sparing lives on the island, yet knowing Sanibel's good fortune meant that people were killed or homes destroyed elsewhere.

By mid-morning, Tomlinson and Dickerson were in a helicopter headed for Sanibel. The plan was to make a low level sweep from Sanibel's eastern tip to as far north as Cayo Costa to assess the damage from the air. They were struck by the devastation to the trees. Dickerson couldn't help but wonder how the rescue teams and damage assessment teams would move around. Both men were encouraged, however, that most structures, at least from the air, seemed to be intact except for considerable roof damage throughout the island chain.

Search and rescue teams and crews clearing roads toiled in the sweltering August heat and humidity throughout the day. City designated teams of roofers were systematically going through neighborhoods, spreading tarps over damaged roofs at no cost to homeowners to minimize water damage. Each structure on the island was inspected for damage by a damage assessment team and given a rating based on the damage. Color coded markers then were placed on the structure, and owners would later be notified of the damage rating and whether it was safe to enter.

The community's spirit surfaced early when the city held its first public meeting for residents in an open courtyard at

Local Nature Checking Out The Damage

Some Needing A Helping Hand

the Holiday Inn on the mainland. The hotel had lost power, like most areas of the city, and an indoor meeting wouldn't be practical. About 400 residents listened anxiously as they heard for the first time that they would not be allowed to return to their homes until the island was safe and the causeway bridges certified for travel by the Lee County Department of Transportation. As she would over the next few days, Zimomra emphasized that safety was paramount. She and Tomlinson outlined three criteria for re-entry: exterior inspection of all island structures must be completed, roads must be cleared of vegetation and debris, and the county must complete inspection of the causeway bridges and certify the structures as safe. Zimomra advised residents that officials would share all information factually and give no estimates of a re-entry date unless they were sure – a statement that placed her under severe pressure all week long. Residents' patience grew shorter and tempers hotter with each passing day the island remained closed. Members of City Council were highly visible at the initial meeting and all subsequent meetings, a tactic that paid large dividends in helping to ease the concerns of residents. The Council had vested responsibility in the city manager and, although it offered comment and support at each meeting, Zimomra was clearly in charge, a validation of Council's well placed confidence in her. Mayor Harrity would say later that was the way the city should run. "The Council should never micro manage a professional like Judie Zimomra." He nicknamed her "Eisenhower" for her handling of the situation. There prevailed a spirit of commonality and purpose at each public meeting, albeit some residents still disagreed with the city's no-access mandate. People naturally were worried about the damage to their properties, but resigned to the fact that they wouldn't re-enter the islands any sooner.

By mid-afternoon 40 law enforcement and National Guard members were patrolling the island. Fish and Wildlife officers along with Marine Patrol and the Lee County Sheriff's Department, crisscrossed the waters surrounding the island to keep anyone from entering by water. Crews were clearing roads, Lee County Electric crews were beginning the reconstruction task and 15-hour days would become a way of life for the dedicated workers.

People who had not evacuated the island were beginning to move about. Officials struggled with the right of individuals to be there, but safety was a real concern; live electric wires were strewn in the streets, unstable trees were still in danger of falling and heavy equipment moved everywhere. Although most residents were cooperative, police found it necessary to bar access where work was being done. In one incident, Sanibel police ordered a couple, walking their dog, off the street

The Original Command Center At The BP Station

Daily Instruction For The Assessment Crew

FEMA With Incident Commander
Tim Barrett

Going Over Plans With Fire Department, Police
Department, City And FEMA

61

where crews were cutting down unstable trees. The pair insisted they had a right to walk their dog where crews were working.

At a 7 p.m. meeting for residents, the city reported on the day's recovery progress. A path had been cleared to City Hall. Heavy equipment was working on major roads to clear downed trees. All secondary roads remained impassable. All utilities were inoperable. A preliminary damage assessment indicated that Gulf front property had been hit the hardest. The best news was, there had been no fatalities or injuries. A building-by-building damage assessment would begin on Sunday, August 15. City Manager Zimomra said that, although Sanibel did not get the storm surge, it now was faced with a "river of vegetation" that must be cleared.

Sunday – August 15
The city calls on all state certified roofing contractors to stand by for work on the island.

Work continued on clearing the islands' roads. Island restaurant owners who were on the mainland were offering the food from their freezers and coolers to emergency people and workers. No electricity meant that food would spoil quickly.

The temporary City Hall at the Holiday Inn became the central point for information. The city had set up information tables and bulletin boards in the lobby. City Council members were always available.

The Unified Command on the island now was operating as a well-organized team. Coordination was required to assure that sections of the electric grid were turned off so that workers were safe to remove trees and debris from the tangled mass of wires and poles. Equipment needs increased or changed moment to moment, and resources had to be tapped to assure that equipment was in the right place at the right time.

The city's Website would prove to be a valuable tool to property owners who were in northern residences or who had evacuated outside the local area. All current information was posted as it became available, including early photos of damage.

Red Cross Arrived Right Away

Island Family Helping To Make Days More Bearable

National Guard Protecting The Islands

Resident Giving Cake To Don Frey, Assistant Fire Chief

The city's 7 p.m. update indicated that 75 percent of roads were clear of debris, and exterior building-to-building damage assessment was 50 percent complete. National Guard and U.S. Marshals, along with Sanibel Police, were operating an island-wide security task force. No access was allowed, either by car or boat. Utilities remained inoperable. Water was not safe to drink unless boiled first. Conditions on the island were considered extremely dangerous with downed power lines, broken water lines and road obstructions. City officials still refused to give a specific re-entry date, but rumors swirled that a firm date was imminent. Tempers flared at the city's refusal to allow residents to return, but the vast majority of people at the meeting supported the city's decision. The city attorney reminded residents that the state of emergency gave the city the legal authority to restrict access to the island.

Monday – August 16

Work crews and damage assessment teams continued their work in the relentless heat and humidity. Many of the island residents who remained were supporting the crews by providing meals and cold drinks.

City Council members Marty Harrity, Steve Brown, Judy Workman and Jim Jennings, along with City Attorney Ken Cuyler, City Manager Zimomra and Police Chief Tomlinson, made their first visit to the island to assess damage. They saw first hand why it was necessary to keep residents off the island until roads were clear.

The city announced a pet rescue and medication- retrieval program. Many people had left pets and medications behind, assuming they would only be gone overnight after evacuating. Search and rescue teams would enter homes with the permission of owners to feed pets and secure medications. A Fish and Wildlife helicopter also dropped medication to people on Captiva who were not yet accessible by roadway.

It was necessary to move the daily briefing to a larger venue. Over a thousand people crowded the auditorium of Bishop Verot High School in Fort Myers for the 7 p.m. briefing. City Manager Zimomra and Police Chief Tomlinson announced to a chorus of cheers that re-entry to the island would begin on Wednesday, August 18, at 7 a.m. Only residents and other authorized people with proper identification would be allowed on the island. Business owners would re-enter at 11 a.m. Residents received a welcome packet of information and guidelines for the re-entry, covering the curfew, mail services, garbage and waste

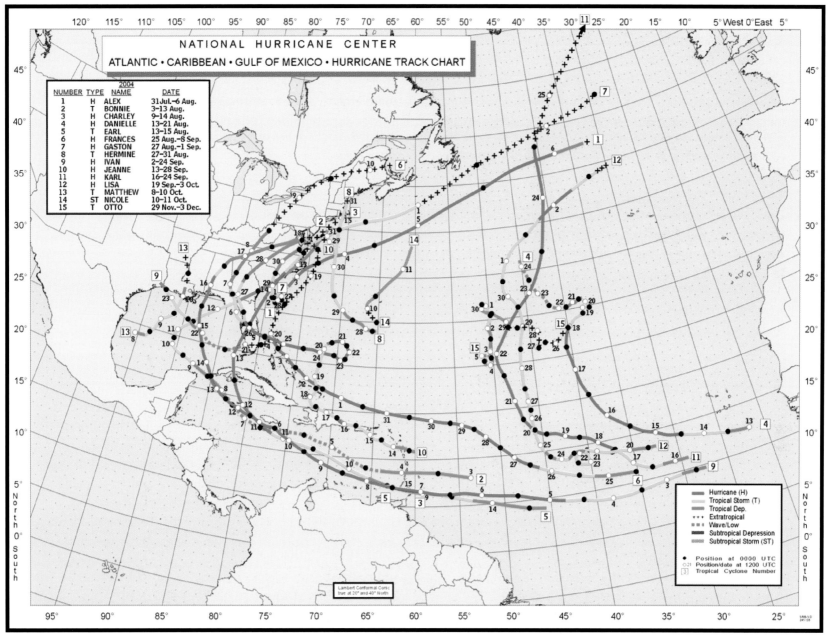

Image Showing The Tracks Of The Storms For 2004

Image Courtesy Of National Oceanographic and Atmospheric Administration (NOAA)

schedules, water usage, construction permitting procedures and a comprehensive list of contractors approved by the city. The mood of the meeting was upbeat. Residents had finally gotten their first concrete information on returning home.

Zimomra would say weeks later "that one of the major roles of government is to inform the public, and that's what we tried to do at all the public meetings we held off island, with our Website and through press releases."

Tuesday – August 17

Residents were introduced to a new way of life when the city recommended a checklist of necessities for re-entry. It included first- aid kit, batteries, bottled drinking water, insect repellent, duct tape, battery-operated lanterns and flashlights and a host of other essentials for life without power, water and basic necessities.

Some stores in the Fort Myers area now were operating on full schedules, though supplies such as ice and bottled water were still not completely available. Discount centers were out of stock on batteries and battery-operated radios. Electric power still had not been restored in many parts of the Greater Fort Myers area. Many hotels and restaurants were still without power, especially those on the west side of the county.

Wednesday – August 18 – Re-Entry Day

In the predawn hours, a trickle of traffic began on the Summerlin Road approach to the Sanibel Causeway. Anxious residents, who for five days had been conjuring images of the damage their homes may have sustained, were heading toward the moment of truth. By 5:30 a.m., a line a quarter mile long already had formed at the toll booths, awaiting the 7 a.m. entry. There was an eerie silence as each additional car coasted to a stop at the end of the line in the darkness, and the engine was shut down. As daylight gradually nudged the mantle of darkness aside, the pent-up anxiety was almost palpable. By 7 a.m., the line extended at least two miles from the toll booths. The cadre of law enforcement officers surrounding the toll booths checked each car's identification as it moved slowly through the gate. Once through the toll gate, residents were met by smiling members of City Council, welcoming them back and waving them through, a welcome home that was a long time coming.

It was truly going back to a world that was different than the one they had left. Most people had no idea of the extent of

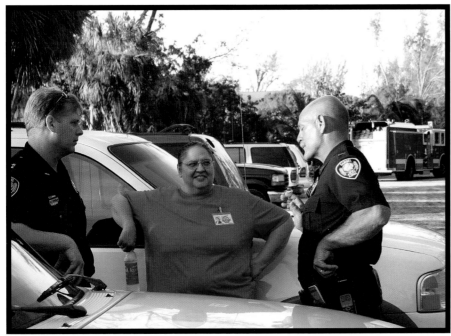

City Manager Judie Zimomra Checking On Progress

LCEC Working Non-Stop To Restore Power

Command And Guard Move To Boat Ramp Area

Iona-McGregor Fire Department Covers Sanibel's East End

damage to their homes or businesses. Officials had said that every structure was standing so no one was expecting a home or business fully destroyed. The early signs of destruction became evident, however, in the downed trees on the causeway's connecting islands and tidal damage to bridges' abutments. A palm tree was standing fully upright in the water 200 yards offshore of the first causeway island, appearing as though it had been planted there years before. From the causeway, Sanibel didn't look much different until one reached the bridge closest to the island. The change in the tree line was obvious. The tall, wispy pines were either gone or in broken piles of debris with tree trunks and huge branches twisted in a variety of grotesque shapes.

Even though city officials had described the destruction of trees on Periwinkle Way, the forewarning did not sufficiently prepare residents for the first sight of the street without the towering canopy. The piles of debris lining the road, tilted power poles and huge decapitated tree trunks were evidence that the main thoroughfare of Sanibel would never look the same again. Houses and buildings that were formerly hidden by trees and dense foliage were clearly visible. The shaded roadway now was open to bright sunshine.

National Guard and police were everywhere. They would become a familiar sight over the next few weeks until the island was open to non-residents.

Residents trickled back into their neighborhoods. Signs of the work that had been done by assessment teams and other agencies were conspicuous. Damaged roofs had been covered with plastic to limit water damage, and homes had been marked with color-coded signs indicating whether it was safe to enter. Many would find collapsed pool enclosures, shattered windows and severe water damage. The August humidity provided a fertile environment for the growth of mold that would be the unseen hazard some would face later. Re-entry day was spent assessing the damage and determining what would be done first. Captiva residents were told to assemble at "Ding" Darling, and they would be transported to their homes since travel on Captiva was not yet safe. They also were not allowed to stay, but had to return to the mainland each evening. It would be several days before they would actually occupy their homes.

Loss of electric power took its toll on fully stocked refrigerators and freezers. After five days, nothing was salvageable and,

Estero Fire and Rescue

Portable Toilets And Wash Stations Set Up
For Residents Return

All Vehicles Check In When Arriving On The Island

Help Arrives From Around The State And Country

in many cases, refrigerators were ruined by the spoiled and rotting food.

Some would elect to remain in their homes without electric power, water or air conditioning. Many would return to hotels on the mainland each night.

RECOVERY

A disaster can bring out the worst and the best in people. Hurricane Charley, unquestionably, brought out the best in islanders. The recovery was a time for not only neighbor to help neighbor, but for total strangers to give of their time, energy and money to help anyone in need. Random acts of kindness were everywhere as the community came together. Refuge Manager Rob Jess would reflect later on how the generosity of island residents, who had provided food and lauded the work crews' painstaking efforts, had touched him.

When City Manager Judie Zimomra first met with other city managers after the storm, they asked what she did when employees hadn't shown up or walked off the job. She told them, "Sanibel had the opposite problem; employees simply refused to leave their post." She had, in fact, become concerned they were not getting any rest and, had mandated vacation time for several employees. Zimomra also stressed the importance of having a plan which had stipulated that, five days before the onset of a hurricane, employees be given time off to secure their homes and families and to rest. "The plan starts with each individual," she stated. "We must be sure they'll always feel secure in their family situation."

Red Cross vehicles circulated around the island serving hot meals. Semi-trailer trucks containing ice and water were parked at the two major supermarkets on the island, Bailey's General Store and Jerry's Market. The commodities were distributed free. Both businesses were dubbed "heroes," according to one newspaper, "for supplying water, ice and food to emergency workers, volunteers and anyone who needed assistance." The few island restaurants that were open offered free food to workers and $2 and $5 meals to anyone else. Jerry's Restaurant estimated they provided over 2,000 meals. The Lazy Flamingo restaurant provided emergency workers with free hot lunches during the five days before residents were allowed back on the island. Even without power, banks opened their doors within a day or two of re-entry and were servic-

Damage Is Surveyed Via Helicopter

Command Directing Efforts; Knows Exactly Where Everyone Is And What They Are Doing

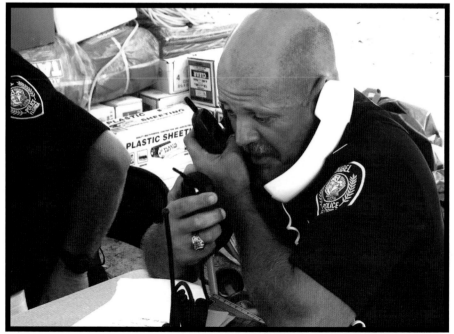

Communications

A Well Deserved Lunch Break That Lasts Only Minutes

Periwinkle Way Before Cleanup –
Department Of Forestry Assessing The Damage

In Front Of Periwinkle Place Shopping Center

Periwinkle Way During Cleanup

Two Weeks After Charley

Clearing Debris Along Periwinkle Way

Restoring Power

ing customers who needed cash or other services. The Kiwanis Club helped churches assist people in need, from giving away food to clearing driveways to cutting trees or any service or item that was required. Two businesses from Naples and one from Fort Myers traveled to the island and set up a free food operation in the Bailey's General Store parking lot. They provided hamburgers and hot dogs to over 1,000 people. Another island business, Schnapper's Hots, gave away free hot dogs even before they were open for business. Donations were taken at the establishment, and almost $1,000 was given to the Red Cross for relief efforts.

One of the clearest examples of inter-agency cooperation came in the form of resources from the U.S. Fish and Wildlife Service being utilized first for the communities of Sanibel and Captiva before they were used for the refuge. All of Sanibel and Captiva's needs were met before any work was begun on the "Ding" Darling Refuge. The refuge sustained $6.5 million in damage, and over 40 percent of habitat was destroyed.

Age posed no barrier when it came to serving the islands' needs. Seventeen-year-old Jimmy Anderson, who three weeks earlier had joined the fire department as a volunteer, was on the island every day at 5 a.m., initially leading National Guard teams in search and rescue operations and later volunteering for any assignment that needed doing. The sergeant major of a National Guard unit observed that it was the first time he had ever taken orders from a teenager.

Islanders entered the world of insurance claims. Insurance companies sent hundreds of adjusters into the area. An "insurance village" was established at the Sanibel Community House as a convenience to residents. As is always the case, a fortunate few settled claims quickly, while others waited weeks and even months without seeing an adjuster. Many would learn that their insurance coverage was woefully inadequate to cover the damage – a result of changes in deductibles and coverage during the 12 years since Hurricane Andrew almost bankrupted the insurance industry in Florida.

Over 3,000 insurance claims were filed on Sanibel and Captiva, but the figure could be misleading. As it happened, many who had damage but did not meet deductibles probably never filed a claim. Residents learned that even though insurance claims were being settled early, getting a contractor to do the necessary work would be another story. Roofing and pool enclosure contractors all of a sudden had a full year's worth of work; estimates for completion or even initial work extended

Original Burn Area Set Up Upon Arrival

Loads Being Verified For FEMA Reimbursement

The Overwhelming Amount of Downed Trees proved To Be Too Much. A New Burn Area Was Established.

75

out for months. The blue plastic tarps that covered damaged roofs were a familiar sight for months following Hurricane Charley.

Moving about became an exercise in frustration. The causeway was closed to all but residents, which meant identification was required at the toll booth. That requirement lasted two weeks from the date of the storm. The good news was that the county suspended tolls. The work on clearing fallen trees continued almost non-stop. With only two main roads, island traffic was constantly stopped to allow heavy equipment to move. The wisdom behind the city's decision to prohibit access to the islands for non-residents became immediately evident. Non-essential traffic from tourists and sightseers would have been a nightmare for cleanup crews and emergency workers and residents. Periwinkle Way was still the focus of the work crews as they labored to clear the right-of-way. The city would later be criticized by some residents for cutting down healthy pine trees, but officials staunchly defended their actions, saying that it was in the public interest to remove the trees from the public right-of-way. Those trees were the culprits in the blockage of roadways and the loss of electric power to the island.

Mountains of damaged aluminum pool enclosures lined the streets. Along East, Middle and West Gulf drives, furniture, refrigerators, carpets and drapes piled up in mute evidence that Gulf front condominiums had borne the serious brunt of heavy water and wind damage. The city's ability to haul the trash away was deeply compromised due to its sheer volume. In order for the streets to be cleared, the city hauled debris to a trash collecting site at Causeway Road and Periwinkle Way to be hauled off island at a later date. The pile of trash eventually grew to several hundred yards long and 20 feet high.

Electric power would come back gradually as Lee County Electric, with 500 line crews, continued their reconstruction of the island's electrical grid. For several weeks the sound of portable generators became the symphony of island life. Lack of electricity forced many residents off the island at night, back to the hotels where they had been staying, for hot meals and respite from the heat. By August 24, 11 days after the storm, 45 percent of households and businesses on the islands had power.

The dedication of city employees was remarkable; they worked tirelessly to restore city services as quickly as possible.

The Lazy Flamingo Opened Each Day For Lunch To Feed Every Emergency Worker That Walked Through Their Doors. The Food Was Hot And The Drinks Were Cold. Thank You!

Sanibel Mayor Marty Harrity lauded their round-the-clock efforts. "It's a case study in how it should be done. We came together as a city in the face of disaster, and at the end of the day it was all about Sanibel and its recovery."

The City of Sanibel estimated that 90 percent of the structures on the island were damaged. Estimates ranged as high as $700 million. That figure excluded damage to utilities, landscaping, roads, city parks and beaches and the thousands of trees lost.

City beaches and the city fishing pier were closed until further notice and would not open for at least 60 days. In an effort to speed recovery, the city waived all building permits for 30 days following re-entry.

By August 29, 90 percent of electric power had been restored, and the water system was in complete operation. The boil water order was lifted. The 9 p.m. to 6 a.m. curfew remained in effect.

Captiva's South Seas Resort, one of the largest resort properties in Southwest Florida, was hard hit by the storm that made landfall close by. The resort announced it would be closed for a year to completely refurbish buildings and the golf course.

The signs of normalcy began to appear as streets were cleared of debris and electric power was restored to many parts of the island. Camaraderie and a sense of humor bound people together. One emergency official would remark to a Sanibel official: "You sure know how to throw a disaster," a comment that would later be immortalized on a T-shirt for distribution to city employees.

Some businesses opened their doors, but with access to the island limited to residents only, local patronage became pivotal. Islanders responded by shopping on the mainland only for those items that couldn't be obtained from local merchants.

There was a collective sigh of relief that the worst was over and things were getting back to normal. But that relief would be short lived...

Check Point To Captiva

South Seas Resort

Captiva Fire Department

South Seas Lands End – Damaged Buildings
And Sand Covered Golf Course

79

HURRICANE FRANCES LOOMS

As residents and the city continued their recovery efforts into the following week, the sixth tropical depression of the season developed in the eastern Atlantic Southwest of Cape Verde Islands on August 24, only 11 days after Hurricane Charley struck. Within two days the depression had built in intensity and now was Hurricane Francis. By August 29, it was a Category 4 storm with winds exceeding 130 miles per hour.

The island was still closed to all but residents. Most buildings still were boarded up and vegetation and construction debris was piled high alongside all roads. Although the pace of cleanup had been feverish, the burn pits the city was operating simply could not handle the volume. Damaged roofs and structures for the most part had not yet been repaired. There was more work to be accomplished than there were contractors, even though the city had short-circuited its usual licensing protocol in an effort to speed up recovery. A strike by a second storm would be even more disastrous than Hurricane Charley had been; hurricane force winds would turn the roadside debris into dangerous missiles.

By Wednesday, August 31, City Weather Consultant Dave Roberts was alarmed at the National Weather Center forecast. It placed Sanibel in the path of the approaching storm. Roberts agreed with the NWC forecast. Although the storm track was more toward Florida's east coast, the worst-case scenario for the islands would be for the storm to make landfall between the Florida Keys and West Palm Beach. Roberts advised the city to once again begin making preparations. Frances was much bigger than Charley, already a Category 3, and potentially much stronger. Forecasters characterized the storm comparable to "the size of Texas." By the next day, September 1, computer forecasting models were in agreement that the storm probably would make landfall near West Palm Beach, cross the peninsula north of Lake Okeechobee and exit to the Gulf in the Tampa Bay area. Roberts then forecast that tropical-force winds of up to 70 miles per hour would buffet the islands.

On September 2, winds from Hurricane Frances had increased to 145 miles per hour. Roberts was now foreseeing winds as high as 100 miles per hour for the islands if the storm held to its predicted path and came ashore north of West Palm

The Beach Was Used As The Main Road After The Storm

Beach. City Council convened a special meeting and advised citizens to voluntarily evacuate the island. Officials expressed concern that recently repaired power lines and the already-compromised structures would be in jeopardy. Damaged trees with weakened root systems also might topple easily. The city extended the state of emergency it had enacted for Hurricane Charley.

On that day a new tropical depression was identified in the south Atlantic. With the track of Hurricane Frances still uncertain and still threatening, islanders had to consider the possibility of yet a third hurricane. The new storm, soon to become Hurricane Ivan, would have even seasoned weather forecasters incredulous at the possibility of another major storm. For residents it meant absorbing the recent trauma of Hurricane Charley, dealing with the impending landfall of Hurricane Frances and coping with the knowledge that a new storm may threaten.

All the precautions for Hurricane Charley were to be re-implemented, this time bearing the caveat that Charley's damage and debris all around the islands could not be overlooked. The psychological effect of the first storm had not yet dissipated. Residents were being faced with a new, more powerful storm, large enough to affect the entire state, no matter where it made landfall.

Evacuating now posed more serious logistics. Before Hurricane Charley hit Southwest Florida, residents fled to the central or east coast. This time, however, residents from the east coast were evacuating westward and already had taken many of the previously available hotel rooms in the Fort Myers area. Some had been sleeping in cars at shopping center parking lots because most hotels were full. For Sanibel and Captiva residents, there simply was no place to go. Many decided to stay put.

The storm track was just uncertain enough to give people pause about evacuating. The fact that landfall was predicted for the east coast also meant that, even if the storm crossed the state, the strongest winds would be somewhat tamed by the time they reached the Fort Myers area.

The city suspended all non-essential operations for four days until the storm had passed. Residents and businesses were once again forced to batten down. Many were in denial that a second storm could strike, but there was no doubting the elevated level of concern.

Captiva Drive After Initial Debris Removal

On September 5, Hurricane Frances made landfall near Stuart on the east coast of Florida where it stalled for several hours, pounding the area with sustained winds of 105 miles per hour. Sanibel and Captiva bore sustained winds of 30 to 50 miles per hour during the course of the day and were subject to heavy rain squalls. Although no damage to the islands was reported, some of the structures previously damaged had temporary repairs ripped away.

Residents clearly had a case of the jitters from the near miss by Hurricane Frances. Both Charley and Frances disrupted the daily routine of cleanup and stirred a low level of nervousness into island life. Suddenly people felt vulnerable. It was hard to plan without watching and waiting for the next weather advisory. The normally tranquil weather that attracted thousands of people to the islands had become a hostile adversary. Anxiety was heightened when, even before Frances made landfall, a new storm was brewing. "Oh no, not again! This can't be happening!" was a common reaction to the weather forecast.

HURRICANE IVAN IS BORN

A thousand miles away, as Hurricane Frances was poised to strike Florida on September 2, Tropical Storm Ivan was formed in the south Atlantic.

By September 4, Roberts was predicting Ivan would gain hurricane strength and move into the Caribbean.

ON SEPTEMBER 15, IVAN REACHED HURRICANE STRENGTH.

On Wednesday, September 7, Roberts' report suggested three scenarios for the storm track, two of which would bring it to South Florida. He predicted the storm would be at its closest point to Sanibel by Sunday, September 11.

On the same day Roberts made his report, a tropical wave drifts from the western coast of Africa to the eastern Atlantic Ocean. With all attention focused on Ivan, the new wave would build in strength over the next week, and soon become Hurricane Jeanne.

Building supply stores enjoyed another rush as residents again stocked up on building materials and the dwindling supply of generators.

7 a.m. Wednesday, August 18 – Residents Return

By Friday, September 9, Ivan has become a Category 5 hurricane with sustained winds of 160 miles per hour and gusting to 200 mph. It is the strongest storm ever to be seen in this hemisphere.

The Lee County EOC extends the local state of emergency to September 14 and triggers another mobilization of emergency response.

In a 9 p.m. meeting on September 10, the City of Sanibel follows suit and extends its state of emergency to September 17. Residents crowded City Hall. The strain was evident on everyone's face. The earlier feeling that it couldn't happen again was replaced by a resignation that, after three consecutive storms, anything was possible. Residents, however, exhibited a staunch determination, perhaps because of the experiences from the two previous storms.

The next day the city called for voluntary evacuation of the islands for the third time in five weeks. Ivan, now a Category 4 storm, had a predicted path close to Southwest Florida.

On September 15, Hurricane Ivan had moved further out into the Gulf and no longer was a threat to Southwest Florida. The next day the storm, now dubbed "Ivan the Terrible," unleashed its fury on the Panhandle of Florida with 130 mile per hour winds, killing 20 people and sending tornadoes crashing through several hospitals and hundreds of homes. Waves grew to 25 feet before smashing hundreds of homes along the coast. Ivan's near miss left islanders reeling from the pressure and imparted a pervading anxiety... anxiety that would be compounded by the next forecast.

"IT'S NOT POSSIBLE...!" HURRICANE JEANNE

Thirteen hundred miles away, Tropical Storm Jeanne formed near St. Croix on September 13, just as Ivan is heading for landfall in Alabama and North Florida.

As Jeanne moved up the east coast of Florida, the islands' weary residents kept a close eye on its path. The previous weeks had

Mosquito Control

Media Interviews Island Resident

A Massive Tree Fell On A Worker The Day Residents Were Allowed Back – He Was Transported To Hospital And Later Released

Signs Pop Up Everywhere

instilled cautiousness about the unpredictability of hurricanes. Jeanne would later prove that caution to be well founded.

Jeanne moved slowly across the Virgin Islands and Puerto Rico into Atlantic waters. The storm weakened briefly, dissipated and then re-formed. It moved slowly to the north over the southeastern Bahamas as a tropical storm, and then guided by a variety of weather patterns, it made a complete loop over the next five days, passing over its own original track, all the while building to hurricane strength. It was now on a track headed directly toward Florida.

On September 24, city weather consultant, Dave Robert, advised the city of the storm's location 600 miles east and that hurricane conditions are possible within 24 to 36 hours. He suggested it was on a path similar to Hurricane Frances.

Hurricane Advisory, September 25

HURRICANE JEANNE IS LOCATED APPROXIMATELY 250 MILES DUE EAST OF SANIBEL. HURRICANE JEANNE IS TRAVELING WEST AT 14 MPH. SUSTAINED WINDS OF 115 MPH WITH GUSTS OF 140 MPH. HURRICANE JEANNE IS NOW A CATEGORY 3 STORM. A TROPICAL STORM WARNING IS IN EFFECT, WHICH MEANS WINDS IN EXCESS OF 39 MPH ARE LIKELY WITHIN 24 HOURS FROM NOW. AT ITS PRESENT COURSE, IT WILL MAKE LANDFALL NEAR OR JUST NORTH OF WEST PALM BEACH AFTER MIDNIGHT TONIGHT.

When Jeanne finally made landfall on Hutchinson Island on the east coast of Florida, it would follow the same path of Hurricane Frances three weeks earlier. Jeanne cut a swath across the state with 140 mile per hour winds. By the time it was just north of Tampa, the storm had weakened to a tropical depression.

Forecasters would later identify an exact location near Bartow, Florida, in the central part of the state where three of the four hurricanes had crossed.

Continued (page 108)

Bank Of The Islands Open for Business

Welcoming Signs of Activity

Good News

Government Ice Brought In From North Carolina – The Driver
Wouldn't Leave Until All The Ice Was Gone

Entry To Island Woods   Island Condo Maintenance

Protected Windows At Lighthouse Cafe

Clean Up Starts

Residents Scramble To Rid Their Homes Of Wet Carpet And Padding Along West Gulf Drive

Debris Piles Up Along Most Roadways

Debris Everywhere

East End Condos Are Emptied So The Drying Out
Process Can Begin

Captiva Cleans Up

After The Storm – Bowman's Beach– Looks Like It Did 50 Years Ago

The Beaches Of Sanibel And Captiva Islands, Still As Inviting As Ever (Bowman's Beach)

Middle Gulf Drive Stripped Of Trees - Three Months After Charley

A Lot Of Work Going On At South Seas Resort

Restoring Brick By Brick

South Seas Resort Mangrove Restoration Project

Bayside Villas, Captiva

Land's End

South Seas Resort Four Months Later – Looking A Lot Better

Captiva Before Charley

Aerial View Of Captiva Drive Four Months After Charley

The Sanibel Lighthouse, The Icon That Reminds Us Of Where We Live

DENOUEMENT

Hurricane Charley's encounter with Sanibel and Captiva Islands was historic in the sense that monetary damage of such magnitude was unprecedented. Had the storm not veered at the last minute, the damage surely would have been many times over what it was. Had the eye of the hurricane passed directly over Sanibel and the predicted tidal surge occurred, most likely there would have been substantial loss of life as well.

Sanibel and Captiva had a hurricane plan, and it was executed almost flawlessly. That plan was tested by fire. More importantly, it worked solely through the dedication, commitment and cooperation of many people and agencies. The 2004 season will be remembered for the damage, destruction and death toll wrought by Hurricane Charley and the ensuing storms throughout the State of Florida. It also will be remembered for the indomitable and resilient spirit exhibited by thousands in communities around the state whose lives were displaced by those storms and yet who continued to rebuild in the face of each new challenge.

For islanders, it was a collectively sobering experience. In hindsight, the main corollary from that summer of fury was the cohesive sense of community spirit that surfaced during and after the storms. And through it all, the true beauty of the islands never changed.

Captiva Beach – Post Hurricane

ABOUT JIM GEORGE AND JIM ANDERSON

Jim George is a Sanibel Island resident and writer for the *Island Sun* newspaper in Sanibel and the *River Weekly* newspaper in Fort Myers. He and wife, Peggy, have lived on the island for 15 years and consider it an island paradise. He felt that the story of Hurricane Charley had historical value and should be told from the perspective of those who experienced it, in the chronological way in which the drama unfolded.

Jim Anderson has been a freelance photographer for over 30 years. His images have captured a broad spectrum of island life and on many occasions have appeared in national and local publications. Jim and his youngest son, Jimmy, were one of the first responders with Sanibel Fire & Rescue in the aftermath of the storm. His photos, most of which have not been published before, captured the essence of the event. Jim, with wife, Sue, raised their three children, Bob, Krista and Jimmy on Sanibel Island.

ACKNOWLEDGEMENTS

We acknowledge with gratitude the contribution of the many people who made this book possible; Peggy George and Sue Anderson for their support, counsel and patience. Our colleagues at the *Island Sun newspaper*, Lorin Arundel, Ken Rasi, Camille Kucaba and Heather Corbin, who guided us through the process of publishing our first book. Friedrich Jaeger and Lauren Davies of *Times of the Islands magazine*, whose cooperation jump started the project. And finally, to all those who shared their experiences, their thoughts and their emotions that gave life to the story.

PERSONAL NOTE FROM JIM ANDERSON

It is impossible to know unless you were here, the tremendous effort that went on the week after Charley. It is my hope that the images will give you some insight into those seven days.

I would like to say how much of an honor it was to work with our Incident Command and all of the Emergency Responders that worked so tirelessly to restore our islands over the week that followed Charley. From the local residents (who should have evacuated) that brought us food and drinks, to the local restaurants that made sure ALL Emergency Personnel had a hot lunch and cold drinks, my sincerest thanks. To the National Guard, many of whom remind me of my own two sons, my greatest appreciation and thanks for your efforts. To our City Officials and City Workers, State and Federal agencies that came together as one, the experience, though I hope none of us will ever have to go through again, was one that I will always be able to say that I was proud to be a part of.

Lastly, I'm especially proud of my two sons. Jimmy, who had just joined the Sanibel Fire & Rescue Squad two weeks prior to Charley, worked 72 hours over six days leading a Search & Rescue team, directed traffic, hauled equipment and went wherever he was needed, which was non-stop. Bob, my oldest son, stayed on Captiva (against my loud objections) and helped to board up local homes and businesses even through the storm. After the storm, he continued to help those who stayed and needed assistance to dig their way out. I would be remiss if I did not also thank Bob for providing us with some much needed humor. It was he and his friend who wrote the infamous message in the sand with 10 foot letters that was picked up by a news helicopter and broadcast literally around the world, which stated: "SEND BEER !"

Back To Normal!